Urban Rebounding™

... An Exercise For The New Millennium

by JB Berns

with Jonathon Flaum

KE Publishing

Disclaimer

This publication is written and published to provide what is believed to be accurate and authoritative information. *URBAN REBOUNDING*™ and its contributors are not liable for any injury and damage that may result from the use of the book or its contents. The book is sold without warranties of any kind, whether expressed or implied, all of which are specifically disclaimed. *URBAN REBOUNDING*™ and its contributors are not engaged in rendering medical or other professional services by reason of developing, writing, or publishing this book. If medical or other expert advice is required, the reader should consult a qualified professional.

TABLE OF CONTENTS

*To my parents, Irvin and Linda Berns,
my two sisters, Beth and Penni,
and my uncle and aunt, Stanley and Rosalyn Kopit
for their constant love and support.*

... An Exercise For
The New Millennium

Introduction

The new millennium provides us with an opportunity for change. It is an occasion to reflect on the necessity of engaging in a deeper and more integrated relationship between body and mind. The system known as *URBAN REBOUNDING* brings together the science of the West and the philosophy and practicality of the East, to form a holistic program of exercise in which people of all ages, sizes, shapes, and states of physical condition can participate.

The book treats the history of exercise in the West as it has unfolded over time, beginning with the Greeks up through the current state of the modern fitness center. Questions regarding our perceptions about exercise are reflected upon and treated in detail. The exercise of rebounding itself is explored in all of its variety: the pioneers in the field, the methods that have come before, their strengths and their flaws.

The science of rebounding is treated in great detail. Clear biological explanations are given as to what it means to do an exercise which literally works from the inside out by strengthening cell walls and cleansing the lymphatic system. The physical properties of rebound exercise are also delved into, regarding the relationship of acceleration, deceleration, and gravity all working simultaneously together on the same vertical plain.

Rebounding for therapeutic purposes ranging from vision correction to osteoporosis are treated in detail, as well as rebounding for the wheel-chair bound. A large section of the book is devoted to photographs of how the *URBAN REBOUNDING* movements are executed. All photos are accompanied by detailed explanations. Throughout the course of the text, testimonies of those who have benefited from *URBAN REBOUNDING* are duly noted.

Finally, and most importantly, the *URBAN REBOUNDING* process is made plain. The philosophy that JB Berns has developed over a ten year period of integrating rebound exercise with the martial art of Okinawan GoJu-Ryu is treated at length. The intersection of Western scientific research and grounded Eastern philosophy is what makes the *URBAN REBOUNDING* program such a holistic and integrated exercise system which brings tremendous joy to those who participate in it. This section outlines the means by which *URBAN REBOUNDING* was developed to meet the needs and expand the range of what can be accomplished in the group fitness setting.

A lengthy appendix describes the method for instructors to become certified in the teaching of *URBAN REBOUNDING*, as well as a section on rebound exercise for the athlete. The appendix also goes over the means by which home use of the *URBAN REBOUNDING* system can best be approached and integrated into one's daily life.

Read on and begin a journey of discovery into the heart of the *URBAN REBOUNDING* system. Your perceptions of exercise will be forever altered and the beginning of doing something truly healthy for yourself, in body and mind, will be within your grasp.

Exercise in Historical Perspective

There is a myth about exercise in the West. It needs to be painful. It needs to be difficult if it is to work the muscles properly. The body, if it is exercised properly, should feel sore and under stress in a day following a "good work-out." It must take a lot of time, and will inevitably, over time, cause stress, fragility, and possible injury to the joints, tendons, and cartilage of the body. These are myths which our culture tends to cultivate and endorse. Why? What is the benefit of promoting such ideas? To answer these questions I will have to first examine the nature and history of exercise as it has developed in the West.

Exercise in Ancient Greece

Athletics and sports have been around in Western civilization since the golden age of Greek civilization. These first progenitors of democracy understood the need for physical exertion, healthy competition, and the maintenance of the human specimen. This classical age valued the perfection of the body as well as the mind. The history of philosophy and science as we know it was born out of our Athenian ancestors. The likes of Plato, Socrates, and, of course, Aristotle, gave voice to a new way of envisioning reality. It is no surprise that this same culture founded the world's first Olympic games. Go to a museum and view a sculpture from fifth century Athens and you will witness first-hand how this "Age of Pericles" sought to understand the potential for the perfection of the human body. The Greeks valued health of body and spirit.

The question then arises as to why, if the birth of Western civilization began in such good health, have we evolved into states of such poor health? The answer is not simple. No answers are simple. Yet, let me briefly analyze the evolution of exercise in the West.

1

Greek civilization marked the first true democracy in Western civilization. This state of reasonable politics was achieved only because Greece enjoyed prolonged periods of peace and prosperity. It was this peace and prosperity that afforded room for the "discovery of reason" in the areas of science and philosophy, as stated above. This period also afforded a flowering of the arts and especially drama in the theatre of Aeschylus, Sophocles, and the famed Euripides. And most pertinent to our discussion here, Greece had the leisure time available to cultivate worthwhile athletic activities—the first Olympics, wrestling, and other forms of sport.

As we in the West can look back to ancient Athenian civilization as a golden age of art, science, and philosophy, we can also recall a golden age of exercise. This was so because there existed a culture which understood the necessity of keeping the human body physically fit and in balance. There existed a culture of enough prosperity and peace, which afforded its citizens the time for physical fitness. However, let us not imagine that every person in Greek culture was physically fit because they engaged in athletic activities. Though democratic for free men, Greece was still a culture that had slaves and viewed women as second class citizens who had no need to engage in sport.

In other words, we must be cognizant that this golden age of exercise was so only for the culturally privileged. Women and slaves maintained their physical condition the way human beings always have—they did intense physical labor which kept their bodies strong. In conclusion, the Greeks who benefited from exercise were the wealthy free men of the culture, not everyone. In looking at the success of Athenian civilization, among other things, we learn that for a culture to engage in exercise which does not involve labor, it must have peace, prosperity, and enough leisure time for the activity.

Exercise in Ancient Rome

This brings us to the next great civilization—the Roman Empire. The Roman Empire indeed possessed all the above characteristics necessary for a culture to have a healthy fitness lifestyle. They were prosperous, powerful, and had an incredible amount of leisure time on their hands. Rome wanted to re-create Greek civilization. Roman scholars translated Greek mythology into Roman religion. They translated the great works of classic Greece into the Latin language of the Roman Empire. Roman artists copied sculpture, poetry, and drama from Athenian civilization. Therefore it should come as no surprise that Rome also mimicked Greece's desire for physical well being. Despite this desire, however, they were not nearly as successful as the Greeks in this enterprise. Why not? They were even more prosperous than the Greeks and had even more leisure time on their hands.

The answer in its full historical context, which I do not have room to go into here, is complex, but the simple explanation is gluttony and excess. Too much power, too much leisure, and too much wealth is not necessarily a good thing. For the Roman empire, it proved fatal. Rather than exercise for the Roman elite, leisure time was spent in heated baths decorated in ornate mosaics. Physical fitness went out of vogue with the rich and powerful, and the drive to please the palate and stimulate all the senses took precedence. Chariot races were the ancient predecessor to the modern horse race. The Roman coliseum became a blood bath where one-time slaves fought to the death as gladiators. It was a place to pit animals against human beings for the sheer entertainment of it. The culture of Rome became fat, slovenly, and brutal. These geniuses of architecture, art, literature, and science lost all perspective when their wealth and power went completely unchecked. The abuses were unadulteratedly grotesque in nature.

In short, the leisure time that a majority of Romans had at their disposal was not used productively as far as exercise was concerned. Time was often squandered at the chariot races and at the coliseum. The citizens of Rome who were probably in the best physical condition were the women and slaves because they performed the majority of the physical labor. Needless to say, the Roman soldiers, such as the famed Mark Antony, were noted to be in supreme physical condition at times of battle. Physical condition was prized as something to be cultivated for violent means—as gladiator or soldier, not as something that provided inner balance and harmony, as the Greeks believed.

Exercise in Medieval Times

After the fall of Rome, the idea of having leisure time to engage in physical exercise was more or less an anomaly. The Medieval period found itself with no outlets for physical exercise. Poverty, hardship, disease, and a life of struggle saw little or no time for leisure. Survival was work. For the most part however, historians imagine that people were in decent physical condition, provided they did not suffer disease or malnutrition. Of course many did suffer disease and malnutrition due to such factors as unsanitary living conditions and poor drinking water. But let us look for a moment on that small segment of the medieval population that did not suffer from disease or malnutrition.

These were farmers who engaged in daily physical labor using their full bodies in their work. These farmers did not sit upon tractors to plow their fields. The majority of them plowed by hand, only the wealthy had horses. They harvested by hand. Built their own houses, made their own clothes, ground their own wheat and cared for their own livestock. These were a working people whose bodies were their daily instrument of sustenance. Without strong and healthy bodies they could not survive for long. As was the case with so many in the medieval period. An almost complete 180 degree turn occurred in Western civilization after the fall of the Roman Empire. The poverty and absence of leisure time for the people of the medieval period lead to such grave demands on the physical body that one could not help but keep in shape.

Exercise in the Renaissance

The period of the Renaissance, with its re-birth of classical culture, brought with it a renewed interest in art, drama, science, med-

4

icine, philosophy and much more. Just as the Roman dramatist, Seneca, would re-write the tragic Greek tale of Oedipus for his Roman brethren; so would Shakespeare go to the annals of the Roman historian Plutarch to come up with the material for his classic Antony and Cleopatra. The cultures of old were re-discovered or literally re-born (*renaissance* means simply re-birth) throughout Europe. A love of the classics along with new developments in philosophy and the sciences. For some reason or other, physical prowess did not take the prominent role in Renaissance Europe as one might imagine. The seventeenth century philosopher and mathematician, René Descartes, and his dualistic understanding of the relationship between mind and body could have a great deal to do with this lack of interest in physical conditioning. The mind was opening, growing, expanding, superstitions were dropping off, but the notion of keeping the body fit was absent.

Nonetheless, this lack of knowledge about the importance of physical conditioning did not hurt the people entirely. For the most part, the majority of the population in the West of the seventeenth century and eighteenth century, worked the land. Like their medieval counterparts, they performed the acts of working the land in such a way that their bodies could not help but keep them in shape. The difference here being that with the opening up of literacy, science, and the arts, the people were simultaneously developing their minds as they worked their bodies. Yet, exercise as such, remained undiscovered.

Exercise in the Modern Age

A good part of the eighteenth century and the majority of the nineteenth century brought the West from the guilded age into the machine age. The industrial revolution was a defining moment for Western civilization when the way of life for the common person would be radically changed forever. A culture that had long been a people of farmers now became a culture of mostly factory workers. The fresh air and the natural flowing movements that accompanied farm work were replaced by the polluted air and the unhealthy repetitive physical movements of the factory. The human body was not meant for assembly line work. It was not meant to stand in one place and use only one particular set of muscles repeatedly. This type of work lead to fatigue and ultimately threw the body out of the balance of its optimum homeostatic environment. Couple this with the fact that factory workers did not have union protection to provide them with an eight hour work day and a five day work week. In the new industrialized economy, many worked seven days a week, fourteen to sixteen hours per day. This work involved standing for long periods with little or no positive anaerobic benefit and perhaps no aerobic movement whatsoever.

Here was a culture with no leisure time, and for the first time in the history of Western civilization, a culture that did not provide the type of work that kept the mass of individuals in sound physical condition. The number of farmers has been steadily dwindling with the increase of factory farming through technological machinery. Less people were needed to run a farm and less healthy physical labor was needed from the few who did operate farms. During this period of industrial expansion, there was little time for exercise. There were some recreational sports, but there was not much time for it. There were also retreats (sanatoriums as they were called), the modern day equivalent of a health spa, that popped up throughout Europe at this time, but these were places only for the very rich. In the United States, similar centers for health and exercise were set up, but these also were for the rich and the often eccentric.

Exercise in the main was something that athletes did, not the common person. As a result, westerners suffered health problems as never before during this period of industrial and technological progress. Cancer, high blood pressure, heart disease, circulatory dysfunction, as well as a variety of neuromuscular disorders that resulted from such an unhealthy and unnatural lifestyle were becoming common side-effects of the modern age.

For a majority of people, there would be yet another major upheaval in their work routine. First it was from the open air of the farm to the enclosed quarters of the factory. Now it would be the abandoning of the standing room of the factory in exchange for the sitting room of the office. This is where we find ourselves today for the most part. Sitting in front of a computer in a cubicle in an office where the air is artificial and no exercise is possible other than that of the fingers going tick tick tick on the key board.

Aerobic and Anaerobic Exercise

The difference today of course is that we do not spend all of our time at work. For the most part we work in an office for eight hours a day and then go home to a personal life. Thankfully, and due in large part to the publishing of Dr. Kenneth Cooper's book titled *Aerobics* in 1968, and his founding of the Institute for Aerobics Research, Americans discovered the need for daily exercise.[1] It only took us a mere 2000 years or so to discover what the Greeks knew in their ancient civilization. We are slow learners here in the West.

The good news for many Americans was that they took the reports coming out of the Institute for Aerobics Research quite seriously. We now had a culture of relative prosperity, power, and a significant amount of leisure time for a large majority of individuals. We no longer had our work to keep us physically fit. Because of all the technological conveniences in the home, we also no longer had our domestic chores to keep us physically fit. We knew we needed aerobic activity to remain healthy and strong, but we no longer had the natural forces of work to engender that physical endurance our bodies craved. Gardening continued to be a wonderful aerobic and anaerobic activity for the body, it was also an activity that has been known to lift the spirits. The problem there was that so many of us lived in apartments and did not have access to a large garden in which to work.

So what did we do for our aerobic exercise in the 1970's and much of the 1980's? Put simply, we ran. To be more specific, we jogged. We jogged on the hard surface asphalt of our streets, pot holes and all. The good news? Many of us got into sound physical aerobic shape. The bad news is that many more of us suffered lower back problems, knee and ankle injuries, torn ligaments, ripped tendons, and shin splints. The physical therapy trade, once only for athletes, now had a completely new clientele due to jogging—the general public. The same is to be said for chiropractors.

As a result of these injuries, those enthusiastic Americans who started jogging, suddenly stopped. Discouraged by injuries, people's interest in jogging never maintained the long term commitment that it was imagined it would in its early stages. In short, injury caught up with the exercise, and people became disheartened and stopped participating in it.

Nevertheless, the medical research into the need for both aerobic and anaerobic exercise was abundant in this period. It was no longer the eccentric who knew that exercise was an important part of a healthy life, this fact was becoming part of the common vocabulary of American life. So we had knowledge, the relative prosperity, and the leisure time, what were we missing? We were missing the appropriate form of exercise for a mass of individuals, none of which who it should be assumed possessed great athletic prowess. Street jogging was a failed experiment on the mass level, though a minority still do engage in the activity—note the several 26 mile city marathons around this nation as evidence. But this is not enough, in truth, street jogging never again had the numbers of people participating in it that it once had in the 1970's and early 1980's.

A fine alternative for a great full body work out of aerobic and anaerobic activity is swimming. Keeping the body in constant movement of all major muscle groups with little stress to bones, joints, and ligaments, swimming makes sense. The problem here is that not all people are swimmers or enjoy the water. Pools are not always accessible and if they are the climate may not be conducive. If one is a swimmer, that is great, but if not, the knowledge of the benefits of this exercise will not be of help.

So then what? The American fitness center to the rescue! Treadmills, Stairmasters, rowing machines, nautilus equipment, and free weights—all there to make individuals healthy, stronger, and to lower their risk of cancer, high blood pressure, and heart disease. And this worked quite well in the beginning of the fitness center movement. Besides all the equipment, there was also a trained staff on the premises to assist the lay person in designing and implementing their own personal work out. These staff would later become known as "personal trainers." People ran, walked, lifted, rowed, etc. at their own pace. Maybe they listened to a walkman while they did it or watched television. But for the most part, though they were in a communal setting, they exercised alone except for the company of a machine.

Over time, this type of activity in itself became boring, routinized, and a habit that many Americans chose not to keep. The committed weight trainer or runner stayed in the gym, but that mass of everyday people who simply wanted to stay in shape, left the gyms as quickly as they signed up. There just was not enough stimulation to keep them there. Exercise became its own sort of factory work—a chore. It was done alone with a machine—it was good for the body, yes, but was it good for the mind and spirit?

As mentioned earlier, it was the seventeenth century philosopher Descartes who created the duality of mind and body in the West. In truth, as we now know, the mind and body are intimately connected and one affects the other. An exercise only for the body but having no positive effect on the mind is an incomplete exercise. Whether Americans knew the reasons for their feelings or not, they reacted in protest by getting off the machines in search of a more human experience to exercise their most personal of all possessions—their body.

In answer to this need, Aerobics was born. The group fitness concept that involved dance-like movements, executed to upbeat music with the aid and guidance of an aerobics instructor. This got people off the machines, brought them into a communal environment and got them moving to music. This was a movement, by and large however, for women. Aerobics has remained predominantly the woman's domain. Let it be said, that for the woman to have such a powerful domain in the fitness arena is a tremendous asset to the history of exercise. The only problem is, it leaves us bereft of fifty percent of the population. But that aside, even for women, Aerobics continues to face major obstacles on the road to becoming an exercise that works.

Problems with Aerobics

Aerobics has conquered the obstacle of workout isolation in the gym, and it should be commended and applauded for such a contribution and achievement in the world of exercise. It has more or less coined the term "group fitness." Nevertheless, several problems ensued, and they were namely: saturation, dissatisfaction with results, and injury. Saturation in that participants could not keep up as the routines became more and more complicated. At one time confident and enjoying themselves, as the world of Aerobics developed, the routines became increasingly more difficult to execute, and as a result many one time Aerobics enthusiasts left the activity feeling discouraged and disheartened. There was simply an overload of routines being taught in classes and participants could no longer absorb the new information, hence, they were saturated with the activity and gave it up.

The second problem was a dissatisfaction with results. Many of the women in aerobics classes across the nation, beyond doing the exercise to maintain weight and keep in shape, were doing the exercise to lose weight. There is no hard and fast rule that says that Aerobics will take excess weight off. It may tone, strengthen, and increase endurance of the participant, but weight loss is not a predictable guarantee. With weight loss being such an overwhelming goal among American women, many, disheartened with their weight remaining constant, left the Aerobics world in a state of disillusionment.[2]

The third problem was the old stand-by that jogging enthusiasts encountered in years prior—injury to the bones and joints. Aerobics is done on a hard surface where the flooring provides no give. The

10

exercise involves a constant pounding to the knees and ankles, causing frequent injury to joints, tendons, and ligaments. These injuries and the soreness associated with them also left many one time Aerobics practitioners feeling too bruised to continue the activity.

These three factors caused a stir in the area of Aerobics, and over time, a solution was proposed: the STEP. Step Aerobics swept across the nation and the world as a new invigorating tool to bring participants back into the Aerobics class. It has been a highly effective tool that solves two of the three above problems. The Step enhances performance and heart rate so it does increase caloric burn and weight loss. The Step aerobic routines are meant to be not too difficult to follow. But what Step gained in solving the first two problems, it drastically lost ground on the last problem—the old nemesis to Aerobics and Jogging —injury. The Step serves to increase the risk of injury, not to decrease it. The height of the Step makes the coming down off of it even more jarring to the bones and joints than regular Aerobics. The general risk of tripping and falling off the raised surface also increases injury risks. And of course there is the lingering problem that though women tend to Step, most men do not step foot inside a Step class.

The next wave of the group fitness dynamic was something called Spinning / Power-Pacing / or perhaps some other brand name you have heard around the gym. Whatever it is called, the nature of this exercise is sitting on a stationary bike and pedaling. It is done in a group, which meets the communal need I mentioned. The movements are not difficult, everyone can ride a bike, so the participants are not saturated with complicated routines. It is non-jarring to the bones and joints since there is no pounding of the legs on a hard surface. Since it does not resemble a dance class in any way, men have come into stationary bike classes in higher numbers.

The problems associated with the group fitness concept of stationary bike training are two-fold. The first is that all the exercise is geared toward the lower body, which can develop disproportionately to the upper body in this case. This can be corrected with additional upper body training, but who has the time? The second problem is more complex, mainly because it is a psychological problem with the exercise as opposed to a physical problem. Put in the most basic terms, the exercise is simply boring. The repetitive nature of pedaling a bike and not getting anywhere is enough to drive many participants to just plain give up the exercise. From the complicated movements of the Aerobics class to the monotony of the cycling class, something was lost. We went from the frying pan to the fire, so to speak. We gave of complication in exchange for boredom, but the results are the same—people lose interest and stop coming to the classes.

Rebounding: A Solution for the New Millennium

This brings us to the present with a lot of questions about exercise. Many experts say simply that exercise, like all other forms of life, is an imperfect entity and will always be that way. Some people will exercise on a machine and will have to put up with isolation. Others will do Aerobics and continue to suffer injury. And still others will stay on the stationary bike and pedal on into boredom. Such is life—we do not live in a perfect world.

What has been overlooked is that exercise is not like life in that exercise is completely scientific and can be studied according to the principles of physics, biology, and chemistry. Life itself is filled with unpredictabilities that are out of our control and that we must simply learn to live with as best we can. There is not a perfect world, but there is indeed a perfect exercise for the human body. This exercise has been studied and endorsed by NASA, the Institute of Aerobics Research, and the National Olympic Committee. Professional athletes have used the exercise for decades as have those who have needed to rehabilitate their bodies. The name of this exercise is REBOUNDING, and the time has come to bring the wonders of rebounding exercise to the general public. My particular contribution is the development of what I call *URBAN REBOUNDING*. Allow me to share with you the reasons why

12

URBAN REBOUNDING is indeed *An Exercise for the New Millennium*. It is time to bring this underground exercise out into the light of day.

Rebounding: The Evolved Exercise 2

Calling rebounding the perfect exercise for the human body may seem a bit presumptuous at first glance. In particular, since I just got through closely analyzing the flaws and benefits of most every other exercise system available. But the perfection of the exercise is simple. When you understand the science behind it you will feel like Sir Isaac Newton did when he discovered gravity while sitting under the apple tree. You too will say, "Ah -ha!," and your perceptions will be forever altered. I mention Newton's discovery for a reason. Gravity, that most natural force was always there—Newton needed only the creative insight to see the reality that everyone experienced, but could not name.

The Physics of Physical Training

To understand rebounding you must understand gravity. You need not be a scientist, gravity is something that is a part of all of our lives which we utilize daily. Put simply, it is that force which pulls every object towards the center of the earth. What goes up must come down. Gravity is why a ball comes down after you through it up in the air. Gravity is the force which teaches all of us how to stand and walk. It is gravity that makes us fall down when we try to take those first steps. In this sense, we learn from gravity how to navigate our existence on the planet. We learn what it takes to stand, maintain balance, walk—we learn all these things by learning how to oppose the natural law of gravity which works to pull us toward the center of the earth.

The very act of the human person learning to stand erect and see the world while standing balanced on his two legs is a testament to the human being's strength. It is the law of gravity which opposes us in our struggle to stand up and walk—and it is gravity which opposes us in every exercise we undertake.[1] There is no greater opposition for any physical activity that a human being encounters besides gravity, so why not utilize this oppositional force in its broadest sense while engaging in exercise to strengthen the body?

Besides the constant force of gravity, there are two other forces which operate in all exercise systems. Be it running, jogging, swimming, playing a game of basketball, tennis, racquetball, or doing a standard aerobics class. The forces, besides gravity, are acceleration and deceleration. Every exercise involves these three forces. Gravity operates on a vertical plane, and in all exercises other than rebounding, acceleration and deceleration operate on the horizontal plane.

Let us take jogging as a prime example. The individual who is jogging, be it on a treadmill or on the street, is constantly working to oppose the force of gravity—this occurs on the vertical plane. At the same time, the jogger is constantly accelerating to run faster and decelerating as they slow down. This acceleration and deceleration are the forces which cause the benefits of the aerobic work out. Put simply, without movement, there is no exercise. This movement happens on the horizontal plane. The feet propel forward horizontally, not vertically. A jogger does not run in direct opposition to the force of gravity, if he did he would be running straight up on the vertical plane. As stated, gravity is the strongest physical force of opposition we face as human beings, so to confront it directly would be the means to accomplish the most efficient form of exercise. Yet all commonly known forms of exercise do not confront gravity on the vertical plane. Most exercise programs deal with gravitational pull the same way as it is dealt with in a state of rest.

Of course this is the case, you think. No person can run straight up in the air and combine the forces of acceleration and deceleration together with gravity so they can all operated simultaneously on the vertical plane and thereby produce the most incredibly efficient workout possible for the human body. Such a feat is impossible, until we all become equipped with our "anti-gravity boots." This has been the received wisdom up to now about exercise. Stated simply, that these are the facts: acceleration and deceleration operate on the horizontal plane in exercise and gravity is on the vertical plane, so it is humanly impossible to experience the full benefit of opposing gravity in our exercise. The two worlds of the horizontal and the vertical planes of our human reality are simply at odds—these are the common sense facts. And this has been true, until the exercise of rebounding solved the predicament.

Harnessing the Vertical Plane

Rebounding is done on a soft surface called a rebounder, a sort of miniature trampoline. The device is approximately 30 inches in diameter and anywhere from eight to twelve inches of the ground. The exercise occurs completely on the vertical plane. The body moves up and down on the soft, non-jarring surface of the rebounder—jumping, jogging, doing sport-specific exercises, as well as aerobic movements. The forces of acceleration and deceleration are at work here just as they are in all other exercises previously mentioned. The difference and unique innovation of rebounding is that like gravity, acceleration and deceleration are also operating on the vertical plane. The force of gravity is wedded together with the forces of acceleration and deceleration as a person practices rebounding exercise. In this way, the force of gravity is enhanced three-fold, and the body taps into the natural force that it has always opposed.

Rebounding is an exercise that uses the natural laws of physics to produce a workout that is more efficient than any other exercise can possibly be. Rebounding is the only exercise whose focus is to incorporate acceleration and deceleration in such a way that they are constantly working to oppose gravity. As the jumping on the surface of the rebounder is sustained, the force of gravity is constantly resisted. There is no exercise whose mode of work is so completely geared to serve this level of optimum energy output other than rebounding.

So we have here a form of exercise which is physically more effective than all other available forms of exercise, not simply because I say so, but because the natural laws of the universe we inhabit make this the case. And though there is arguing with opinion, there is no arguing with the law of gravity and its operation in relation to the human body and its work output. In their 1980 study, NASA determined that rebounding is 68% more effective an aerobic exercise than jogging.[2] This effectiveness was determined according to the use of G-Force (gravitational force) which NASA finds of particular importance when training their astronauts for the weightless experience of space flight. My look at the NASA research will be covered in further detail in chapter three, which covers the history of rebound exercise.

A Bonus: The Reduced Risk of Injury

With the above being the case, you would think the simple science of the situation would clearly make rebounding the most desirable form of exercise available to people. Do not people want to exercise in the most efficient way possible? Do not people want to burn the highest amount of calories in the least amount of time with the least amount of energy output possible? If people want to do these things and exercise in a way that is scientifically intelligent as opposed to a way that is simply difficult, than rebounding is definitely an exercise worth learning more about. Thus far I have established the bio-mechanical and physical superiority of this exercise, but there are other factors to consider. Injury, for example.

In the other exercises surveyed in the previous chapter, injury was a major factor in determining their unsuitability, and a major reason for declines in participation that the exercise experiences over time. Does this effective exercise known as rebounding include a lesser risk of injury? The answer to this question is a resounding yes! According to a study done by the University of Oklahoma, the soft surface of the rebounder produces an effect which absorbs 87% of the shock to the system of jumping up and down.[3] Forget about shin splints, knee and ankle problems, or problems with joints and tendons. The soft forgiving surface of the rebounder, besides being so efficient in its utilization of all properties involved in bodily exertion (acceleration, deceleration, and gravity), is also the safest exercise around. This shock absorbing effect of the rebounder on the legs also translates to a highly reduced risk of injury to the neck, upper back, and that most often problem area—the lower back. The shock to muscles, joints, and bones is almost completely eliminated, thereby allowing you to exercise for longer periods of time with great comfort. This way, strength and endurance increases without having to sacrifice the health of the knees, lower back, and neck.

Jumping for Joy

Everything that can be done in an Aerobics class can be done on a rebounder. The difference is that on the rebounder the jarring effects to the body of repeatedly jumping up and down on a hard surface will be completely eliminated. Following this line of reasoning, it is clear that rebounding is the most logical exercise to participate in according to the natural scientific laws we live within as human beings, and at the same time, it is the safest form of exercise for how our human bodies are constructed. Fine, you say, we all know broccoli is good for you, but it does not mean that fact makes you want to eat it. Science and statistics are one thing, but the enjoyment of human life is another. People want to do an exercise that is enjoyable, more than enjoyable, they want to do one that is all out fun.

Now here comes the really good part about this exercise—it is simply a joy to do and it makes you feel fantastic while you do it and after you do it. There are clear, specific, and detailed scientific reasons for this which I will cover in later chapters, but right now I want to look at the common sense reasons why rebounding is such a natural way for people to enjoy themselves while they exercise.

What was one of the first things you remember naturally loving to do as a child? For many people the answer is simple—they loved to jump up and down. To flaunt with ultimate joy their temporary victory over the natural force of gravity. As children we so often went into happy fits of literally "jumping for joy!" It was how we expressed our fascination with reality, our natural love for this world that in our innocence we were constantly discovering for the first time. And if you ask these same adults where they loved to jump best, the answer is resoundingly clear—they loved to jump on a soft surface. The surface was most often a bed, because that was all that was available. But for many, they were given access to truly express this emotional and physical joy by being introduced to the wonder of the trampoline. For so many children the trampoline opens up an entire new world of self-expression. It is the freedom to soar unfettered while landing safely and unhurt. The trampoline is that rare sort of device which allows for the wonder and curiosity within the child's heart and body to ultimately bounce forth into the open.

Ask these same adults, who speak about jumping on a trampoline as children, when the last time they have been on a trampoline. They cannot tell you when the last time was—they cannot tell you the last time exercise was such a liberating joy as it was to jump on the trampoline as a child. People are surprised to learn that these memories of joy which so many thought only to be a childhood recreation, was actually the most efficient form of exercise in which the human body can engage.

As with so many other things in this culture, when we become adults we too often forget the wonder, excitement, and awe in which we viewed the world as children. A child naturally knows what makes them feel good both physically and emotionally. Their sense of innocence and wonder keeps them closer and more properly attuned to the needs of their body and mind. As adults, we become encumbered with the "shoulds" of our culture and we too often forget how to simply listen to our own internal wisdom about what we need. Our culture has been telling us for thirty years that we are not getting enough aerobic exercise and we need it. As a consequence we seek to do the responsible adult thing and exercise. Children instinctually know that the body needs aerobic exercise except they do not call it exercise, they call it playing.

Too many adults in this fast-paced culture of deadlines and constant communication have forgotten the magic and relief of simply being able to play. There is no more incredible activity for a child to play then jumping on a trampoline. As an adult, why should you be left out? Why should you continue to view your exercise as work rather than as a thing of joy which will help you to re-discover your child-like spirit? There is no longer any reason to do it—the time to jump for joy has returned. It has actually never left, and was always there for the asking. The beauty is that you can now satisfy two equally important needs simultaneously: exercising and having fun. Our culture too often creates unnecessary dualities. Children at play are having fun and there is no practical attribute to simply having fun. Adults, on the other hand, must be responsible hard working individuals who participate in exercise because it has practical end results not because the activity itself is fun. If an adult only did an activity because it was fun, he would be called "childish." These are cultural myths which we need no longer embrace.

The activity of rebounding is fun and it has incredibly practical results when done regularly. Fun and practicality exist side by side in the activity of rebounding. If you must, you can justify your adult preoccupation with practical results by fully understanding the science of rebounding technology. Even if you forget some of the scientific principles, you can simply experience the enhanced sense of well-being, the weight loss, the increased stamina, balance, and coordination—and from this you can satisfy the need of your practical adult mind. But the true beauty of this exercise is how much it resembles "child's play," it is an activity that will keep you laughing from the raw joy of it. In this culture, fun is not much of a justification for "exercise," but you can keep it to yourself if it makes you uncomfortable to keep exercising for the simple fun of it. After all, as an adult you should be thinking about high blood pressure, cancer, free radicals, and heart disease. I have thought of all of these things and will explain rebounding's superior handling of them throughout this book. But, with all that aside, what will keep you jumping is the joy of it. If you have forgotten this fact, just watch a child and be reminded ever so quickly of what I mean. Imagine, there is finally an exercise that actually takes the simple facts of the human condition into account.

Prisoners of the Machine

According to the parameters I set up in the first chapter, I still have two other important criteria by which to judge the exercise of rebounding. The communal aspect of the exercise with relation to the special program of *URBAN REBOUNDING* will be discussed in detail in chapter 6, and merely touched upon here. The focus I will stay with and pursue however, is that of the isolation of individual and machine as they relate in this century, particularly in the present.

As discussed in the first chapter, it was the machine that first took the human person out of a daily routine that involved a natural working environment which promoted health and wellness. The fresh air and hard work of a farm operated without the high-tech machinery of today's corporate factory-food producers, was and is the best physical fitness center imaginable. The constant movement of the body coupled with connection with the land that enhanced the life of the mind and spirit made farm life a more natural one for the human person to exist within. The body was intimately connected with the change of season, the production of food, and the general interrelationship between human being and the environment of nature.

We talked about the industrial revolution as the major force which changed this cycle of living and produced a more regimented one where people were cut off from nature and thereby removed from a part of themselves. Removed from a part which made them healthy and free individuals. They now had to punch the factory clock, be on factory time, and abide by factory rules rather than their own. In this atmosphere the human being was no longer working in concert with the direct connection of sustenance according to the laws of nature, but was instead forced to conform to the economic necessities dictated by the demands of factory production. This loss of freedom and personal autonomy had an adverse effect on the body as well as the mind.

In the beginning of this industrial revolution it was thought that the human person would control the machine, but in fact things worked out to be quite the opposite. In fact, the machine would inevitably control the human person. The pace of factory production was based on the speed of the machines not on the rhythms of the human body. The human person was forced to align their productivity, pace of work, and posture to the demands of a machine.

It was thought that the machine was there to make the human being's life easier and healthier, but unfortunately, such was not the case. Let me take a few examples from the industrial age, I will then continue on with the analysis into today's information age. My reasons for making these digressions are in a sense twofold. First, I want to establish the pattern of how machines can adversely affect human life, and how an exercise machine is an apparatus which only serves to perpetuate this adversity. Secondly, I want to demonstrate why the rebounder is an evolved piece of exercise equipment which will return to us the simplicity of an exercise which superiorly meets physical as well as the psychological needs of our human condition.

Let me first look at a rather simple example—the common farm tractor. At first, this machine was thought to be a great achievement and one of the most natural utilitarian uses of the internal combustion engine. And with this, things began rather innocently. The common farmer was able to now take the burden off his horses, which he had traditionally used for plowing the field. The farmer could work more efficiently, plowing straighter rows, and plowing more acreage in less time. The negative effects seemed small enough at first—a modicum of increased pollution on the farm due to the exhaust fumes of the tractor. But production was increased significantly, and it was production that was valued above all else with regard to the economic expansion which accompanied the technological developments of the industrial revolution. But with this piece of equipment, like so many other machines of the modern-day, what started out as something to be utilized to make the farmer's life better and more prosperous, turned out to do exactly the opposite in the long run.

At one time the United States had more farmers than anything else. More persons working outside for themselves, according to their own laws and to those of nature—it was this sort of independent freedom on which the United States was founded. Today, however, less than three percent of the population of the United States works as farmers. And of that dwindling number, the majority are working in technologically generated environments guided by principles which the factories of old were founded upon.

The human person became the prisoner of the very machine which was initially seen as its liberator. How did this happen? The tractor became more advanced over time, it got bigger, combines were introduced and the farm would forever change. Whereas a person on his own with horse could reasonably care for 10 acres of farm and sell products locally, an industrialized farm could afford to care for 5,000 acres of farm and sell products internationally. The sheer volume of sales in product from such a factory style farm allowed for it to completely under sell the family run farm. The result is the family run farm went out of business, unable to survive in this competitive machine driven market.

In this situation the human being became alienated from their work, from their body, and from the peace of mind that work once provided. Let me look at a further example of this industrial age and the alienation it has caused with regard to our furniture. There was once a time when everyone had custom made furniture constructed from start to finish by the hands of a craftsmen. This craftsmen understood the wood, knew its grains and its textures, knew the way to join pieces of it together so that it would remain bonded for several lifetimes. The dovetail joint, the mortise and tenon—each piece of furniture had an individual character, it was made by a human to be used and enjoyed by a fellow human being.

There was a care involved, a notion of connection not only to the craft, but to those that it served.

But this all changed radically with the advent of factory milled furniture created cheaply to serve the mass of an anonymous public. The wood used was not even real—particle board, press board, and other synthetic materials were introduced. To achieve even the natural look of a wood grain was a deception achieved by the gluing on of a sheet of formica made to look like wood grain. One time craftsmen were transformed into factory workers with ear plugs who could not hear themselves think while they worked, let alone have the freedom to enjoy the beauty of their task. Mass machine production meant that the machine controlled the pace, product, and quality of the furniture—the "human element" was reduced to having as little importance as possible.

A craftsman is alienated from his work and the object created is no longer a human object created by individual hands. It is a foreign object, and that alienation is felt when it is used for a writing desk or as a chair to sit down on to have a meal. It may not be felt consciously right away, but over time, the notion that in the modern world, the majority of us are surrounded by objects created by machine and not by humanity, makes us too feel less human—more alienated from our natural selves.

Alienation in the Computer Age

The information age has not been much better on this score, in fact, many would argue that it has been much worse. The computer for example has been that machine that was supposed to free us from futility and tediousness. Like the many machines of the industrial age it was supposed to be the item that would make our lives "convenient," and leave us the time and freedom to spend our lives on the meaningful things—like family, relationships, learning, culture, and of course exercise and the outdoors. In its inception, the personal computer was meant to do those menial tasks which no one wanted to do. It was meant to be the absolute servant of the human being. But yet again, over time, the computer has become

25

the master of the human being.

Today, one's whole life is on the computer, bank records, hospital records, even library records, as ironic as that may be. Even that one bastion of literature, the library, that is not electronic and does not require a hard drive to be able to read something from it, even this place has your records on computer. More and more, children are being taught by computers. These minds of innocence and openness are being flooded in their earliest years by electronic images teaching them how to read or count. These same computer and CD-ROM games will later teach them how to kill via the video game, but this is another matter entirely. The point being that the most basic learning has become depersonalized in our culture. It is not good enough any longer for human beings to teach human beings, we now need machines comprised of wires and circuits to teach human beings. It is too soon to tell what the ultimate results of these things will be, but I would venture a guess that alienation from the human experience will be par for the course.

The adult world which was once so dominated by the factory floor is now dominated by the computer work station. One is isolated in a cubicle with a machine. A machine whose pace dominates the work experience the same way the assembly line once did. There is no longer the time to write a careful letter, or to have the peace to sit back and read one with the paper in your hands. Electronic mail delivers messages across the world in a blink of an eye, and immediate responses are sought. These conveniences are supposed to give us more leisure time, but instead the human work pace is simply picked up to keep up with the speed of the computer. The natural needs of the human being are not accounted for, what matters is serving the speed of the computer because doing this service will increase company profits. So once again, the machine does not serve the human person, but the human person serves the machine.

The pager/cell phone phenomenon is but another example of the frantic pace of technology putting the human person under an inordinate amount of stress which they were never meant to endure. The pager/cell phone is yet another of these conveniences which are supposed to make people more accessible and make communication easier. But on the contrary, these forms of communication have left no rest for the weary. The pager/cell phone makes it impossible to leave the office at the office. People are now working out of their cars, they get called at lunch, when they are with their families, and when they are taking a walk in the park. These are not surgeons or emergency room physicians, these are every day people trying to run to keep up with the pace of technology. Communication and the flow of information is constant and endless, but what of importance is being said?

Rebounding: A Human Solution

Now, what do all of these factors have to do with exercise. It is very simple. We live in a society where the machine too often controls the life and pace of human life. Why should our recreation be so guided and controlled? Why should our time for exercise be but another experience of alienation where the only point of contact for the human person is a machine? Do not we spend enough time in our cars, on the phone, eating food cooked in the microwave, and working with the computer as our closet co-worker? Why not spend that special personal time doing something as positive for yourself as exercising without the interference of a machine?

When you shut the computer off why go to the gym and turn the stairmaster or treadmill on? Why go from one technologically controlled environment to another? Is there not some space in the daily routine of human life that is free from the encumbrance of the machine which drives you at its pace rather than the natural flow of your own? I believe there absolutely must be, and I see rebounding as one of those liberating human spaces where you can become yourself again. An exercise in which you can use your own body and the natural law of gravity. An exercise which will bring back the singular joy of the childhood memory of jumping up an down because you simply could not contain your excitement and your wonder with being alive.

Rebounding is not an ultimate panacea to the stresses of modern life. There is no such all encompassing antidote—only the proper attitude and lifestyle can begin to bring the remedy we seek. Nevertheless, it has become clear to me that rebounding on a regular basis can become an integral part of developing and cultivating a lifestyle which brings us closer to our natural homes. The rebounder is designed to serve the needs of the human body. It is the human person which determines the pace of the exercise, none of which is filtered through an electronic machine.

Like a child, you simply jump up and down and feel the movement of your body as it overcomes gravity by doubling its G-force on the deceleration stroke of the jump. No machine is needed, no plug in, no fancy contraption. All that is needed to spring into shape is the rebounder, this circle shaped device which is like a mini-trampoline. The various routines, exercises, and explanations are in chapters to follow. But for now what is important to understand is the freedom this exercise affords. You can take the rebounder to the beach with you, you can have it in your office and take it out and jump for ten minutes when you are feeling stressed, you can bring it on a business trip, you can have it anywhere.

I call my program *URBAN REBOUNDING* for several reasons. In regard to what we are discussing here, the reason is quite simple. We are an urban society, the world does not travel backward, the furniture craftsman and the small farmer will probably not return on a broad scale ever again. Those times have passed me by, and I accept that, though I do not put it out of my mind entirely. I remember it warmly and am cognizant of it as I contemplate rebound exercise and its meaning for the human person. Urban life can be a strain of infinite number where the human person is continuously under the pressure and control of the bureaucracy and the machine.

In the midst of this urban context, I want to offer an exercise which can be done comfortably within the urban environment, yet at the same time, can temporarily lift you out of it, at least in mind. Unlike the Western philosophical tradition begun by Descartes, I do believe that the mind is interconnected with the body—that there is in fact no duality there. By exercising the body through the course of rebounding, you will also be exercising your mind in a way you never knew was possible. Rebounding is an exercise which brings an outlet to the stresses of urban life which I feel is ultimately necessary for the health of the body and spirit. This is not to say that someone who lives in the country cannot experience the joy and fulfillment of this exercise. Quite to the contrary, I am simply saying that I have conceived of a program with the stressed urbanite in mind.

So, there is an exercise which is scientifically superior to any other, is non-jarring to the body, and is not psychologically alienating, but rather will restore the body and mind. So what is this exercise all about? How was it discovered? Why has it been kept a secret for so long? What is the internal science behind this full body work out? Read on and meet the answers to these questions and discover more about this exercise for the new millennium— *URBAN REBOUNDING.*

The History of Rebounding

Rebounding has been around in a variety of forms for the better part of this century. The term "rebounding," however, was coined less than thirty years ago by the true father of this form of physical exercise, Mr. Albert E. Carter. For the better part of two decades, Mr. Carter has led a single handed crusade to bring the wonders of rebound exercise to the general public. He has written two books on the topic, several articles, and has conducted seminars throughout the world. Much of this chapter will be a recollection of the trail that Mr. Carter has blazed in the field of rebound exercise. I do that for two reasons: first, I want to pay homage to the individual who first made me aware of this incredible exercise, and second, tracing Albert E. Carter's trajectory goes hand in hand with better understanding rebounding as it is known today.

Since Albert E. Carter's influence, many other individuals have come on board to the discipline of rebounding, and have made their various contributions to its evolution. I use the word evolution here for a distinct purpose. Nothing is born out of a vacuum. Necessity is indeed the mother of invention, and I want to make clear that *URBAN REBOUNDING* is not an exercise system that comes out of nowhere. It is rather a refined and distinctive methodology born out of utilizing the research and experience, not only of my own, but of these valuable contributors that have come before me. I feel that this exercise has been progressively evolving to meet the needs of individuals of all shapes, sizes, backgrounds, and limitations. I see *URBAN REBOUNDING* as an important marking on this evolutionary chain. I feel it imperative that this point in the exercise's journey be appropriately marked within its historical context. I want to make it clear that I mean not to bring you a new fad that will be discarded when the next one comes along. Instead, I mean to show you how this exercise, which has been around for a long time, has progressed, and why it is now in the perfect modality to be utilized by all. Fads come and go in popular culture, be it in the field of exercise or anything else. I present to you a tried and true system of exercise which I have found the means to hone and shape into a totality which I know will add to its process of evolution.

Roots of an Exercise

With this said, let me proceed to look at rebounding's colored and fascinating history. Before Albert E. Carter came on the scene there were some starts and stops, but no true forward movement in this entity which we now call rebounding. The ancestral cousin of the rebounder is the full size trampoline. The sport and recreational use of the trampoline is noted by the *Gains Book of World Records* as coming into common usage in the year 1911.[1] George Nissen, the founder of the Nissen corporation, the sole manufacturer of the trampoline in its early years, is credited with being the definitive impetus behind the sport of trampolining. It was Nissen who perfected the manufacture of the sturdy trampoline in 1936, this is the model with which most of us would be familiar. For years, trampolining has been and continues to be a competitive gymnastic sport. It has also been utilized as a recreational activity for children. However, the idea that this activity could somehow be therapeutic was not made abundantly clear until Albert E. Carter laid the groundwork for it.

Nevertheless, though the healthy effects of rebound exercise were not well documented, the sheer enjoyment and positive feelings that came from trampolining lead to an eventual production of smaller personal units. The first such unit was developed soon after George Nissen had put his full size trampoline on the market. Two years hence, in the year 1938, Ed Russell created a sort of mini-trampoline. Excited with this new development and hopeful of its potential sales with the general public, Mr. Russell brought the prototype to an advertising agent named Victor Green. Before truly understanding the nature and reason for the creation of this device, Mr. Russell hoped to acquire the necessary tools from Victor Green to allow him to turn a profit. When this result did not occur as quickly as Mr. Russell hoped, he soon abandoned interest in the project and probably moved on to his next idea. Victor Green, however, maintained interest in this curious piece of equipment that Ed Russell had introduced to him. So curious, that in the intervening years Victor Green implemented a series of changes to the structure of the device that added to its solidity and practicality. Pleased with these modifications, Mr. Green filed for a patent, and held exclusive rights to the production of this device until 1975.[2]

It was this year, 1975, that the U.S. patent office finally insisted that Mr. Green allow his manufacturing techniques to become part of the public record. This was done so on July 1, 1975, by the U.S. Patent office. Mr. Green was President of Tri-Flex Manufacturing, Inc., a company which produced these mini-trampolines units out of Houston, Texas. Mr. Green's firm built rectangular shaped units with the specifications of 45 inches in length and 33 inches in width. Word of the therapeutic and physiological effects of rebound exercise was spreading on a limited basis at this time and two more companies sprang up in 1975. One of the companies had the sole focus of producing rebounders to be used as therapeutic tools to aid in the correction of poor vision. The name of this company was the Leffler corporation, and they worked out of Portland, Oregon. In the chapter on therapeutic rebounding, I will explain in detail how the rebounder can be utilized for vision improvement as well as a slew of other physical problems.[3]

Another company in Houston, Texas got underway in this year, 1975, they were called the Trampa company, and were the first to produce rebounders for the sole purpose and intention of physical exercise. It was Ed Anderson, owner and President of the Vital Corporation, who designed the first circular shaped rebounding units. This by the way, is the most efficient shape for a rebounder and marks a significant development on the road to creating this optimal exercise. It was this same year, 1975, which the first public seminar was held to demonstrate and discuss the use and benefits of rebound exercise. This presentation, which took place in Seattle, Washington, was lead by Gerald Hinkle, President of the Trimway corporation, the latest entrant into this budding industry of rebound designers and innovators.[4]

It was this same year that Albert E. Carter was finishing up his two year national tour with the professional team of trampolinists known as the "Gymnastic Fantastics."[5]

Carter was all over the country performing acrobatic tricks and feats of strength on a full size trampoline. He had been a professional trampolinist for twelve years prior, and a three time amateur champion. Well known for his trampolining excellence, Mr. Carter was asked to write an article on the health benefits of rebound exercise. With multiple corporations producing these units throughout the country, it was felt to be a necessity that an expert in the field should testify to its health benefits. It was under this circumstance that Al Carter was asked to write an article on the health benefits of rebound exercise. After much research and investigation, Carter published his findings which were then re-issued in a small pamphlet called *Rebound to Better Health*, published in 1977. It was at this time that Carter coined and trademarked the term *Reboundology* as the science and study of rebounding and set up the center called The National Institute of *Reboundology* & Health. This center has been providing the exercise community for decades with the leading and newest developments on the research of this exercise.[6]

Such was not always the case. In the beginning, all Carter knew was that trampolining had served and strengthened his body and that of his fellow trampolinists in ways that other exercises never could. He had his own experience and the testimony of others to go on as evidence that rebounding is a superior exercise, but experience alone is not enough, and Carter knew this. He needed scientific research to back up his claims, and with the goal of finding such research, his quest begun.

Carter was a sort of one man crusade to unearth any and all

studies that had been done on the nature of the physiological benefits of exercising on a vertical plane on a soft surface. He published
his findings in two subsequent books, *The Miracles of Rebound
Exercise* (1977) and *The New Miracles of Rebound Exercise* (1988).[7]
As we all do, Carter stumbled from one area to another, finding bits
and pieces along the way, but nothing definitive. Unlike most of us,
however, Al Carter persisted and came upon findings that surprised
even himself.

NASA Comes Onboard

Better than he could have imagined, Carter was put in touch
with NASA, and told that they use an equivalent to rebound exercise to train and prepare their astronauts for the condition of space
travel known as weightlessness. Rebounding is also used by NASA
to provide astronauts with increased vitality and regulation after
they return from space. NASA provided Carter with reams of valuable information and research conducted by their own scientists.[8]
This research was conducted by the Bio-mechanical Research
Division, NASA—Ames Research Center, Moffet Field, California
in collaboration with the Wenner-Gren Research Laboratory,
University of Kentucky, Lexington. This initial
cooperative report was chronicled in the *Journal of Applied
Physiology* 49(5): 881-887, 1980. The four scientists who conducted the study were A. Bhattacherya, E.P. McCutcheon, E. Shavartz,
and J.E. Greenleaf.[9]

The initial study conducted which proved to NASA that
rebound exercise was so effective was conducted with a comparison
test of rebounding to the effects of jogging on a treadmill. A group
of physically fit males between the ages of 19 and 26 were studied
while alternatively using a rebound device and a treadmill for physical conditioning. The study required the subjects to walk, jog, and
run on the treadmill at four different speeds as well as jump on the
rebounding device at four varying heights. The two key points that
were discovered in this study and that are quoted here, first
appeared in the *Journal of Applied Physiology* as follows:

1. "...for similar levels of heart rate and oxygen consumption, the magnitude of the bio-mechanical stimuli is greater with jumping on a trampoline [rebounder] than with running, a finding that might help define the parameters needed for the design of remedial procedures to avert deconditioning in persons exposed to weightlessness."

and

2. "The external work output at equivalent levels of oxygen uptake were significantly greater while trampolining [rebounding] than running. The greatest difference was about 68%."[10]

This second quote is a rather simple one to understand. It means simply that with the same work output from the body, the energy efficiency could be up to 68% greater while rebounding than jogging or running. It is for this reason that I call rebound exercise the most efficient exercise available, and why I feel it imperative to share these results with a wide audience. To understand the first quote we need to comprehend a thing or two about the conditions of weightlessness. Not that I imagine I am writing for future astronauts, though some of you may have that ambition, but because weightlessness is directly related to properties involved in rebound exercise.

NASA engaged in this study in the first place because they were searching for a new and more efficient mode of physical conditioning for their astronauts. They found that space flight was causing a bizarre condition in its participants—they found that when the body experienced weightlessness for a fourteen day period, bone and muscle mass was known to shrink in size up to about 15% of its standard mass.[11] The natural logic of the body simply adjusted to its environment, and without the law of gravity in place, the muscle and bone mass did not need to be as strong. To maintain equilibrium in the body, the body mass actually began to adjust itself to its new environment. This is fine if one means to live out there in space, but if one wanted to return, a way of stabilizing body mass was needed. After conducting the study, NASA claimed that "...averting the deconditioning that occurs during the immobilization of bed rest of space flight, due to a lack of gravireceptor stimulation (in addition to others factors)." [Recovering from space flight] ..."requires an acceleration profile that can be delivered at a relatively low metabolic cost." And since the scientists found that "trampolining [rebounding], as long as the G-force remained below 4-G's, the ratio of oxygen consumption compared to bio-mechanical conditioning was sometimes more than twice as efficient as treadmill jogging."[12]

On a rebounder the rate of exercise is constantly below 4-G's, therefore these results remain consistent across the board. So what is NASA saying to us? They are saying quite simply that they have found an exercise which compensates and rehabilitates an individual who has undergone the most difficult stress to their body that is imaginable (leaving the natural forces under which the body is designed to exist.) So if this exercise is good and efficient enough for individuals undergoing these extreme conditions, why not reap the benefits for yourself in your own daily life?

Albert E. Carter did not stop with NASA. He also went on to provide findings of a study done under the auspices of the United States Air Force. Major Ward Dean, M.D. found that the athlete in top physical condition can establish a maximum of 3.24 G's while on a standard rebounder.[13] This study confirmed the viability of the NASA study, thereby making it clear that the efficiency of rebound exercise proposed by NASA would remain constant across the board due to the findings of G-force variation.[14]

Scientific Study Validates Rebounding

As I mentioned previously, one of the best benefits to rebound exercise, in addition to the efficient and holistic workout, is the non-jarring effect on the bones and joints thereby providing a safe, effective, and ultimately sustainable workout. The watershed study of this non-jarring effect of rebound exercise was undertaken by the

University of Utah. A. W. Daniels, Ph.D., Professor of Material Science and Engineering and Orthopedic Surgery conducted at study at the University of Utah which compared the load bearing effects of jogging to rebounding. He concluded the following:

"Determined the approximate spring constant of the rebounder by measuring the deflection of the surface when various persons of known weight stood on it. It was found that the constant was 770 lb/ft. Calculated the length of time of impulse load contact for a typical 165 lb person running on a rebounder, and on a wooden board track where the constant was 33,000 lb/ft. The time of contact is inversely proportional to the impact force. The calculated times of contact were .13 seconds for the rebounder and .02 seconds on the wooden board track. Since .02 is only about 15% of the .13, the maximum impact force on the rebounder would be only 1/6th that of the wooden board track."[15]

Once again, this scientific study helped confirm what rebound enthusiasts have been experiencing for years: a smooth unobtrusive effect on bones and joints. Not only was the efficiency of the exercise well documented (by NASA), the consistent G-force ratio tested (by the U.S. Air Force), to ensure consistent results, but now the undeniable safety of the exercise was recorded by this University of Utah study. With this, rebound exercise and Albert E. Carter were well on their way to becoming a phenomenon of exercise knowledge which could easily be put into practice by anyone who had an open mind and was willing to try rebounding for themselves.

The Phenomenon Hits the Road

Now proven, Albert E. Carter took these findings on the road to discuss them and perform various rebounding techniques for large groups of physiologist, athletic trainers, and physicians. One such meeting was at the National Health Federation convention, in Anaheim, California. It was here that Carter first came into contact with Olympic Trainer, Dr. Harry Sneider. Dr. Sneider had been following the innovative developments being made by rebound exercise, and he developed a program of exercise which he felt could improve the desired results several fold. Harry Sneider called this method *Aerobic Resistive Rebounding.*[16] This simple yet brilliant innovation introduced the use of light sand weights (one to three pound) into the rebounding routine. Participants would simply hold these weights in their hands and move their arms and legs in established, routinized motions. Harry Sneider's method caught on and he wound up introducing *Aerobic Resistive Rebounding* to exercise guru Jack Lalanne, who began to incorporate it into his own exercise routine. Dr. Sneider also trained 1979 Mr. Universe, Mike Kentzer, with this resistive method, as well as Olympic athlete, and American high jump record holder, Dwight Stones. Stones had trained for two years consistently on a rebounder before his amazing display in the 1984 Olympic games.[17]

A study was implemented by Albert E. Carter in which he sponsored an engineer to look at the effects of this other kind of rebounding developed by Harry Sneider, known as *Aerobic Resistive Rebounding.* The step by step results are as follows:

1. "If one stands still on the rebounder and holds a one pound weight in each hand, it will exert one pressure on each arm, a total of two pounds on the trunk and legs."[18] I am starting from ground zero here in describing how the physics of this resistance training on the rebounder works. For this first step, all we need to understand is that here the rebounder responds like a common scale. Go to the Doctor's office and get weighed, remain on the scale and take hold of the eight pound bowling ball the nurse hands you. You will weigh eight pounds more. It is the same thing on a rebounder. Stand still on it with a weight in your hand, and your body weight will increase by whatever the object held weighs.

2. "If one jumps on a rebounder creating a 2 G Force, the weight will create 2 pounds of force at the bottom of the bounce on each arm; a total of 4 pounds on the trunk and

legs."[19] It is a fact that when you jump on the rebounder and create a force of 2 G's (which you will with a standard jump), you will double your weight. It follows, that the weights also double in weight when a 2 G force is created. So, let us take the scenario of a 165 lb individual jumping on the rebounder creating a 2 G force, the individuals's weight will increase to 330 lbs, thereby creating a natural tension which exerts maximum energy efficiency.

3. "If one creates the bounce by rhythmically moving the weights in the hands forcefully up and down, the G force is at least doubled again at the bottom of the bounce and 1 G of deceleration at the top of the bounce. This subjects each arm to an additional five pounds of resistance, or a total of 10 pounds."[20] In this effect we see that rebounding is not only the most efficient aerobic exercise available, but it is also an incredibly efficient anaerobic exercise. The strength training of the G-force coupled with the use of weights in controlled motions produces an excellent strength training workout. This combination produces an amazing cross-training effect. In this way, Harry Sneider and Albert E. Carter had anticipated the need of cross-training by at least ten years. The *Aerobic Resistive Rebounding* routines that were developed did indeed function as a cross-training system that was ahead of its time.

4. "If one moves the weights from the shoulders to the waist while sinking into the mat six inches and bouncing off the mat six inches, the weights in the hands move upward a total of approximately 2 feet each bounce."[21] This step is merely a means to understand how the formula works as we proceed into the next step. The formula to measure the work output produced is equal to weight times distance; with this in mind let us examine the next step closely.

5. "Assume one bounces six inches off the mat 100 times in a minute, moving the weights 1 foot in a curl exercise. That

40

would be moving 10 pounds x 2 feet x 100 times, or 2000 foot/pounds of work in one minute...or, if you used 2 pound weights with the same exercise, it would be 4000 foot/pounds of work...or, if you used the three pound weights, 6000 foot/pounds."[22] I have now established the combined system of the cross-training routine of aerobic and anaerobic exercise on the rebound unit. We know that the six inch movement on either end of the bounce equals a 2 foot output, we also know that the combined G force at the bottom and top of the jump make a one pound weight act like a ten pound weight (a 2 pound weight act like a 20 pound weight, and a 3 pound weight act like a thirty pound weight), multiply this formula times the repetitions and we have our work output. It seems difficult to fathom that this exercise can be as efficient for the body as it is, but the physics of it are clear and the results speak for themselves.

6. "For the purpose of illustration, let's assume that you use the two pound weights moving them an average of one foot while sinking six inches into the mat and bouncing six inches off the mat. You complete the Daily Dozen (a series of exercises shown in *Harry and Sarah Sneider's Olympic Trainer*), 25 repetitions, 3 sets. It takes you twenty minutes. This would be the equivalent of moving a 40 ton freight car 1 foot in 20 minutes, or a Volkswagen up to 40 steps in 20 minutes, or curling a 100 pound barbell in twenty minutes."[23] These measurements are calculated without including the factor of body weight, let us look at this last step to conclude the analysis.

7. "Assume you weigh 150 pounds and are bouncing high enough to create 2 Gs. At the bottom of the bounce you weight 300 pounds. Your entire weight is moved upward 1 foot 100 times a minute x 20 minutes, or 600,000 foot/pounds."[24] The efficiency is accounted for by utilizing gravity to its maximum benefit by accelerating and decelerat-

41

ing on the vertical plain. It is the rebounder which does the bulk of the work for you, and the beauty of this is that your weight training, like your aerobic workout, also becomes a self-contained, innovative, and exciting program. Rebounding gives you the best of both worlds without the hassle of having to use free weights or standard gym equipment weights. Like the comparison with jogging for aerobic activity, performing anaerobic training on the rebounder provides minimal injury risk, a decrease in soreness to the muscles, and a maximum efficiency quotient for the entire body.

With Harry Sneider and Albert E. Carter both working diligently to spread the word of the physical properties of rebounding and the astounding results it produced, Dr. Kenneth Cooper's Institute of Aerobic Research wanted to get involved. They did so by conducting a study of their own in 1981. The study was conducted by Dr. Larry Gettman, Ph.D., Paul Ward, Ph.D. and R.D. Hagan, Ph.D. Their study concluded that "strength gains[when rebounding in between circuit weight training] showed a 25% improvement over standard circuit weight training."[25]

A Slow Journey into the Spotlight

So with all of the success of rebound exercise in the early 1980's, why have you not heard about it until now? Why have not rebounders replaced treadmills, bikes, and Stairmasters in physical fitness centers across the country? Or, minimally, why does not rebound unit usage at least rival this aforementioned equipment? The answer to that is more complicated than one might think. A scientifically proven exercise program is not enough to ensure its spread and mass success. Economics often stand in the way of things that are actually good and logical to use becoming available as a quality product for the mass market. This is the glitch that so adversely effected the rebounding market in the late 1980's, and to better understand the evolution of how we have gotten to where we are with this exercise, we need to comprehend this predicament.

In 1977 there were only five rebound manufacturers, this remember was at time when the general public was just becoming aware of the health benefits of regular exercise, let alone rebounding. Nevertheless, there was a certain intrigue with the novelty of a rebounder, or a mini-trampoline, as so many referred to it then. This developing interest in rebounding had more to do with the device as something for recreational use than it did as something for the health benefits that experts knew existed. However, this recreational usage of the rebounder was enough to ensure a consumer demand. This consumer demand created a need, and suppliers were in competition to meet this need. By the year 1981, there were over one hundred United States companies that manufactured rebounding units of varying shapes, sizes, and qualities. Most of these companies wanted to provide the consumer with some sort of literature about the health benefits of rebounding with the device they purchased. As a result of this need for literature and rebound education, Albert E. Carter and the National Institute of Reboundology and Health Inc. steeped in and provided their services. Newsletters, flyers, and manuals were produced and sold in large quantities to companies that sold rebounding equipment. In this way, the Institute was slowly integrating its revolutionary ideas about exercise into the mass market, and the goal of better educating the public about rebounding was becoming realized. It was a pinnacle of rebound exercise in this country and things looked like they would only grow from this point.[26]

Things change however, it is one of the only things in life that we can count on—its state of flux. And such was the case with how well rebound manufacture and education material dissemination was being handled. When established retail chains with large corporate offices behind them saw that there was money to be made in this budding industry, things began to unfold. Five of the finest rebound manufacturers of the time reported that they had all secured contracts to produce units for the a certain major national department store, which I will refer to here simply as "store-X."

43

This was misinformation however, they had all not secured contracts, they had merely been granted the opportunity to bid for the contract. The results were fairly predictable, the companies went into strict competition with each other as they vied for the coveted national account. Store-X did choose just one manufacturer, not the company with the highest integrity and highest quality product which afforded maximum safety, maximum health benefit, and maximum durability, no. Store-X, knowing little about the actual purpose of this unit, simply picked the company which produced the rebounding unit at the lowest cost. A low wholesale price would lead to them being able to sell the rebounder to the consumer at a cheap price. This is what the consumer wants, they figured,and perhaps they did...at least in the short run.[27]

A & B Products won the national contract for store-X by producing a rebounder which they billed as one dollar per square inch. So a 36 square inch round rebounder wholesaled for $36.00, which was unbelievably cheap, even for those days. But though A & B got the coveted bid, even they could not produce the rebounder at this cost. They lost $2.27 for every rebounder they manufactured and were soon out of business. Despite this, consumer demand for rebounding units remained high, and J.C. Penney, Sears, and other national department stores took note of Montgomery Ward's enterprising sale of rebounders, and they too got in on the action. The demand to keep the price low was strong, but no United States manufacturer felt they could manufacture the rebounder at a price these national chains wanted, and maintain any sort of quality. But this fact did not stop the national chains from giving their consumers what they desired.[28]

As has happened with several other industries, the national chains simply went overseas to have rebounding units manufactured to the specifications of their desired price. Without knowledge of the science of what made rebounding the exercise that it was, overseas manufacturers simply focused on producing units at the cheapest cost, using the cheapest labor to produce them by investing in the most inexpensive materials. In the beginning, the results proved to be a true achievement for the national chains. They now had a variety of products which they could sell retail to the consumer for $39.95, then $29.95, and eventually as low as $19.95. And with the cheap price, consumers bought rebounders in droves. In 1982, 72 million dollars was spent on rebounders, and in 1983 that figure increased by an additional 33%. Price wars raged as the competition continued, and in a very short time almost all United States rebounding manufacturers went out of business. The only companies to remain were those that manufactured for those who understood the wonders of rebound exercise long before the mass market craze took over. By 1984, 78% of all rebounding units manufactured were sold by large retail chains. Only a rapidly diminishing 13% of all rebounding units sold in that year were constructed by U.S. manufacturers.[29]

Cheap rebounders were available on every corner, but the public's fascination with these devices were true fad, and the integrity of rebound exercise was denigrated. The cheap manufacture lead to the units breaking and being unsafe, which translated into many consumers hauling their rebounders to the town dump or simply to the front of their house for garbage collection. The department store chains also had no interest or need of providing their consumers with information about the health benefits of rebound exercise. The result was that the National Institute of *Reboundology* and Health, Inc. had no market for the distribution of its multiple sources of literature regarding rebound education. It was at this time that Albert E. Carter temporarily shut down his office in the United States and accepted an invitation to do some rebound education in Australia, where the phenomenon was first catching on.[30]

Carter's excursion to Australia proved fruitful. He gave seminars, conducted classes, and made several media appearances throughout the country. It was a reinvigoration for the Institute and provided hope to Carter that the integrity of rebound exercise would remain intact, even if this meant pursuing its demands in a different country than his own. This was a successful venture all around and the opportunities of rebound education and development once again produced a feeling of boundless possibility.

The Hong Kong Connection

It was amidst this feeling that Carter's presence was requested in Hong Kong. He was summoned by Peter Daetweiler, the Chief Executive for the Holiday Inn Corporation of the South Pacific region, as well an active player in Hong Kong politics. Daetweiler, had been an avid runner for many years and always maintained top physical condition. But after a time the constant running was giving him knee trouble to the point where his pain necessitated the need of cortisone shots. This situation was untenable for Daetweiler and he needed a new exercise. Someone introduced him to Carter's *Miracles of Rebounding* (1979) and it changed his life. He was able to exercise again without the pain and he felt better than ever. He wanted to express his gratitude. But this was not all. Daetweiler was also a businessman and a politician and he saw a way that rebounding could help repair a citywide crisis. You read right, Daetweiler was convinced that Albert Carter and his rebounding miracles could solve a city wide dispute.[31]

The City of Hong Kong was embroiled in a labor dispute and an impending strike threatened from the Police and Fire Patrol forces. Given the dense population of Hong Kong, such a strike would have violently disrupted order and safety throughout the city, and was to be avoided at all costs. The bone of contention between the government and the Police and Fire patrol unions was exercise. The city felt exercise to be imperative, and therefore instituted a program in which Police and Fire safety workers were required to maintain a regimen of jogging at least three times a week for thirty minutes and working out with weights on the days in between. The government also insisted that this regimen be done on the worker's own time. The unions felt exercise was important but had two problems with the government's stipulation of how the exercise should be practiced. The first problem, as they saw it, was that if

46

their employer required them to exercise then they should be allowed to exercise on government time. The other problem was that many Police officers and Fire patrol workers complained of knee problems which made jogging untenable.[32]

The government felt that a workout on company time was completely unrealistic. It took time for the worker to get changed, go to a running track, run for a half hour, shower, and return to their post. For the government, this was simply too much time spent off the beat/alert status while the workers were being paid as if they were performing work related duties. The situation came to an impasse, and disaster seemed imminent. It was at this juncture that Albert E. Carter was called upon to work his "miracles." Carter met with the chairman of the Urban Council of Hong Kong, Cheong-Leen, and with the help of Daetweiler a resolution to the conflict was underway.[33]

Carter gave a demonstration of rebound exercise and presented the scientific data to support his claims. He then went on to explain that the Fire and Police workers could rebound three times a day for ten minutes each time and achieve the full physical and psychological benefit of an intensive exercise program. The obvious benefit was of course the much decreased risk of injury, and the workers with knee problems not having difficulty performing this exercise. But even more than that, the workers could perform the exercise on company time without ever having to leave their post. With moderate aerobic and anaerobic rebounding for ten minute sessions, significant sweating is not a problem, so there would be no time lost to shower and change clothes. The forgiving nature of the soft surface is so forgiving on the muscles and joints that one could perform rebound exercise without stretching before hand, thus no additional time for stretching would be needed. Rebounding is a vertical exercise, not a horizontal one, so one can do it while remaining in the exact same space. It could be done in the fire house, on the police post, in the office, wherever. All of these factors convinced Cheong-Leen that he had in fact found the remedy they so desperately needed. The police chief and fire chief were called in, they tried the rebounders, heard that they would be allowed to use it on company time, and agreed to the terms. The strike was averted and a major crisis in Hong Kong was avoided.[34]

All Hong Kong needed were the rebounders, so Al Carter called the six manufacturers he still knew to be in business at this time. He ordered a few rebounders from each manufacturer and multiple use tests were performed by the Police and Fire Department workers. The bad news, as Al Carter feared, knowing what had happened to the rebounding market, was that all the rebounders tested did not hold up under the conditions of high numbers of workers using them on an hourly basis. Cheong-Leen contacted Carter in a panic, maintaining his hope and commitment to the exercise, he was concerned with equipment. This executive took it upon himself to fix the problem. He assigned Carter three of Hong Kong's top structural engineers and asked Carter to explain the science of rebounding to them so they can produce a superior rebounding unit that can be utilized by the work force at large.

A deadline of two weeks was given to come up with a model, and a second deadline of only another two weeks to manufacture 20,000 units. Needless to say, there was an extraordinary amount of pressure to come up with the right unit. In addition to the engineers, Carter was also assigned to the head of the Sports and Recreation department. This was done so he could train the head of the Sports and Recreation department as well as his staff of teachers to properly teach this exercise to the workers, so maximum efficiency could be assured.[35]

Carter met with the engineers in the mornings and the Sports and Recreation department in the afternoons. Things went quite smoothly, and in a rather short time things came together. Some lasting truths were developed about rebound construction that helped to re-ignite the exercise. It was determined once and for all that the round rebounder is the best possible shape to ensure strength and durability. It was determined that the rebounder should be exactly eight inches off the ground. This allowed for a 300 pound individual to achieve maximum height and G-Force without ever being concerned of grazing the rebound mat to the floor. It also allowed a 6' 2" individual to jump without the worry of hitting their head on a standard eight foot ceiling. The right material for the mat was found, the appropriate spring materials, they even discovered a way to manufacture the rebounder so it can be folded when it is not in use. This allowed the unit to be completely portable and definitively met the requirement of rebounding being able to be done on the job. With a portable rebounder, officers were able to bring it out to their post like a briefcase. Convenience and durable construction went hand in hand to produce a superior piece of equipment. The lessons that were learned under the stress of the two week construction period continues to serve the rebounding industry today as an event marked as an engineering breakthrough.[36]

The rebounders were manufactured on time and the Police and Fire unions were happy with their new exercise. When the results got out to others in the Hong Kong public and to other agencies, rebounding was the talk of the city. Dr. Charles Low, the chair of the Physical Education department at the University of Hong Kong, made it his business to ensure that at least half his staff members were trained to teach rebounding. Rebounding became so popular in such a short time at Hong Kong University, that it seemed that everyone was doing it. Before an exhibition match when John McEnroe was playing in Hong Kong, the University of Hong Kong's Women's tennis team performed a choreographed routine on rebounders which got resounding cheers from the capacity crowd of over 4,000 spectators.[37]

Nursing homes, civic organizations, schools, hospitals, everybody wanted rebounders and the knowledge of using them to go with it. Al Carter worked with a staff to get rebounding literature translated into Mandarin, Cantonese, as well as several local dialects. The appetite for this innovative approach to exercise was without limits, and once again, the National Center for *Reboundology* and Health was in full swing. It seemed that the sensibilities of the Eastern approach to physical well being and preventive medicine made the populace incredibly open to exploring alternative methods of exercise.[38]

Rebounding Flourishes Overseas

The success in Hong Kong of rebound exercise lead to an invitation to Mr. Carter from the Marcos's to visit the Philippines and to demonstrate rebound exercise. The year was 1983, and Carter first met personally with the Marcos's and their physicians. The meeting led to a gathering of over 200 members of the medical community getting together to hear about and see rebound exercise. The meeting turned out to be a tremendous success and once again the word spread. Rebounding was being demonstrated in health fairs on the streets of Manila, and an office called Rebound-Dynamics was established, and yet again, another country was convinced of the amazing qualities of this exercise.[39]

Though rebounding flourished overseas, the negative experiences of consumers of the early eighties lead rebounding to become a sort of underground exercise in the United States. Not many people knew of the amazing health and therapeutic benefits, and those who did were often considered to be on the fringes of what was accepted by mainstream exercise practitioners. Nevertheless, Carter did eventually return to the United States and serve these rebound enthusiasts on the fringe quite well. By this time, other holistic health experts who valued the quality of what they knew of rebounding began to promote its effects. These experts all brought valuable contributions to the field, contributions which continue to enliven this one of a kind exercise system. Let me look at some of these contributors that have been working to bring knowledge of rebounding to the general public. My aim is to make you aware of what is out there on this topic and how *URBAN REBOUNDING* means to build upon it.

U.S. Experts Endorse Rebounding

Worldwide motivational speaker and personal consultant, Anthony Robbins, has not done the research on this exercise, but has felt its effects and endorses it strongly in his book *Unlimited Power*, he writes: "[T]he best all-weather aerobic exercise is trampolining [rebounding], which is easily accessible and puts minimal stress on your body...There are many books on trampolining [rebounding] and how it strengthens every organ in the body. Please take the time to pursue this life-enhancing form of exercise. You'll be glad you did."[40] With the amount of people Robbins reaches with his books and tapes I know that he is responsible in part for the resurgence of interest in rebound exercise in the United States during the 1990's.

Many of you may know Marilyn Diamond from her now famous recipes in the vegetarian *Fit For Life* cookbook. Diamond is one of this country's leading authorities in the areas of nutrition and holistic health. In her all encompassing *Fit for Life II: A Complete Health Program* book that she co-wrote with her husband Harvey Diamond, they express their wonder and gratitude with the discovery of rebound exercise.

It is so simple and convenient a means of exercising the entire body that many people tend to think "How could something so easy and fun be so good for you?" If it were a bit more complicated, more costly, or caused greater discomfort, it would probably be more popular. The fact is that Resistive Rebounding will probably revolutionize the fitness movement in the next decade, not only for world class athletes but for everyone interested in fitness, from the weakest to the strongest, from the clumsiest to the most fleet of foot....Rebounding is probably the best all-around exercise you can get.[41]

The Diamonds go on to present a workout which was developed for her book by the renowned expert I highlighted here, Dr. Harry Sneider, the creator and supreme teacher of Resistive

51

Rebounding. Diamond also notes the cellular workout that rebounding supplies, this leading to a clean and healthy physical body inside and out. This is a topic I will cover in full detail in the next chapter.

Dr. Morton Walker, a renown expert and author in the field of holistic medicine has made his contribution to the field of Rebound Studies with his illuminating book entitled *Jumping for Health* published in 1989. Walker details case study upon case study of persons therapeutically healed from engaging in rebound exercise, I will touch on many of these subjects in the therapeutic rebounding section of this book.

Bruce Fife, N.D. wrote the renown best-seller titled simply *The Detox Book* and published in 1998. The subtitle of his book is "how to detoxify your body to improve your health, stop disease and reverse aging." His book includes chapters on food, diet, fasting, juicing, as well as a chapter on exercise detoxification. It is not surprising that the exercise he recommends is rebounding.

The most amazing detoxification exercise is without a doubt rebound exercise... Rebound exercise provides all the benefits of ordinary exercise plus many others unique to rebounding. As a form of detoxification no other exercise comes close. The reason rebound exercise is so good is because it works the entire body, not just the arms or leg muscles.

Rebound exercise does not just strengthen the muscles, but it strengthens every single cell of the body, both muscle and non-muscle. It strengthens the bones, cartilage, joints, and every organ of the body. The liver, pancreas, kidneys, brain, etc. all are subjected to the increased gravitational force of rebounding and will respond by growing stronger. In so doing, they build up increased resistance to disease. As a result, all of the systems and organs of the body function more efficiently. If the organs work better, they can also remove toxins better.[42]

As you can see, the word about rebounding for physical conditioning, strength training, and internal health has gotten around. Bruce Fife's book stands as the latest popular work on this subject. I will go into depth about the nature of the cellular benefits of rebound exercise in the next chapter. Thus far, I have meant to lay the groundwork for explaining why this exercise works aerobically, anaerobically, and is so beneficial for the body and mind. Much of what follows in the next chapter is biology as opposed to the physics I have thus far been discussing, but nevertheless, I am confident that the connections will be clear and easy for you to understand.

Rebounding: The Right Exercise at the Right Time

The desire to find an all inclusive aerobic/anaerobic exercise system coupled with the desire to improve internal well being, has brought back a renewed interest in rebounding in the late 1990's. We have become a culture obsessed with health, aging, and exercise, and we are constantly searching for new ways to improve ourselves. Note the hundreds of fitness magazines, the health clubs, cookbooks, diet books, and self-help books on the market. Too often the solutions to difficult issues are presented prematurely, and the results are discouraging.

Fortunately, rebounding has been around a long time, and though it may be new to you, it is definitely not new. The question may now arise, which is a completely legitimate question: "With all this great information on the market about the miraculous effects of rebounding, why do we need another book about it?" I answer this in two ways. First, never before has all the cumulative research and history of rebounding been brought together and made available in one complete source. Secondly, and more importantly, I bring a new dimension to the field.

URBAN REBOUNDING is a phenomenon which has drawn on the work of all the experts, yet has revolutionized the exercise into a system befitting the needs and requirements of today's individual. As wonderful as rebounding is, if people are not doing it, they cannot benefit from it. The model of *URBAN REBOUND-*

ING has got people out there rebounding again in a way that has never happened before on a mass scale. The unique modality of rhythm, pre-choreographed fluid forms, the motivational and integrated instruction, and the focus on joy in movement is creating a swell. *URBAN REBOUNDING* has begun to do what Marilyn Diamond predicted in her book ten years ago, it is starting to "revolutionize the fitness movement."

URBAN REBOUNDING is the means to bring rebounding to you in a way that is fun and that will keep you doing it for a lifetime. I am building on all the knowledge that has come before me, adding to it, and have refined it into a system that makes you want to do it. Many have said that once they tried *URBAN REBOUNDING* there was no way they would ever go back to any other form of exercise, which when compared with *URBAN REBOUNDING*, seemed lifeless and mediocre.[43] The physics and biology of rebounding was always clear to us. The only uncertainty was uncovering why absolutely everybody was not participating in it if it was so effective. The answer was multifaceted of course, but when I broke it down one thing seemed clear—the humanity of the exercise had not yet evolved to match its scientific superiority. People needed motivation, change, challenge and the opportunity to intentionally explore the body/mind relationship. *URBAN REBOUNDING* provides all of this and more. Read on now as I explore the internal science of rebounding.

The Internal Science of Rebounding 4

As I move from the outside to the inside of the body, it is important to understand why rebound exercise is of such value for the entire human body. I call rebounding the most efficient form of exercise available because it is a full body work out. By full body I do not mean that it simply works the abdominals, triceps, biceps, pectorals, etc. as say, something like weight training does. Also, I do not mean that because of its aerobic effect, it simply works the heart and lungs. I actually mean that it works the entire system of the human body, inside and out.

There are two main aspects to the internal science of rebound exercise. One refers to what I call cellular exercise, and the other refers to the cleansing of the lymphatic system of the body. I will first look at cellular function and rebound exercise and then discuss the lymphatic system, its function in the body, and how rebound exercise aids this function.

Cellular Function

The body is made up of an average of anywhere from 60 to 75 trillion cells. Every muscle, piece of tissue, skin, organ, joint, etc. is made up of cells. The exercise of rebounding works to simultaneously strengthen every cell of the body. From internal organs to skin tissue, as you bounce you reinvigorate and rejuvenate your entire system.[1] The beauty of it is you do not even have to think about it, your cells do the thinking for you.[2] Sounds too good to be true, but like most real truths in life—it is a simple thing. It all goes back to that universal law which is the key to this exercise—the law of gravity. Remember the foundational principles of how this exercise works. It is the only exercise where all three physical forces of exerted motion are simultaneously operating on the same plane. Acceleration, deceleration, and gravity act together on the vertical plane while you bounce on the rebounder. The cells adjust natural-ly to the conditions of exercise. For example, the cells in the calf muscle of a person doing leg lifts become stronger due to the expe-rience of gravitational opposition. During rebound exercise, the cells interpret acceleration, deceleration, and gravity, together as a triple gravitational force, and thereby naturally adjust to become three times as strong. Because gravity works on the same vertical plane with acceleration and deceleration as you rebound, the cells of the body experience all three forces as forces of gravity. The result is a strengthening and conditioning of the entire body, cell by cell.[3]

In this way, the term full body work out takes on a whole new meaning. In his book, *The Gravity Guiding System*, Robert M. Martin, M.D., states:

A human can, with intelligence, solve the problem of grav-ity in his environment in a way completely unavailable to four-legged animals or apes. The force of gravity on his backbone is not along the horizontal length, but instead is compression on a column when he is sitting or standing. His vertebrae, with the respective intervertebral discs, perform better in a flexible, vertical column than when acting as a movable, seg-mented, horizontal structure like that of a quadruped's spine...Is it not possible that the spinal column of man is basi-cally more adapted for vertical weight bearing than for hori-zontal weight carriage?[4]

Dr. Martin asks us this question rhetorically of course, he does in fact believe that the human body is better adapted to the vertical plane. Dr. Martin's research aids us in understanding why not only is the vertical plane exercise of rebounding beneficial to our internal system via the cells, but is better for our skeletal structure via our spine. This is what is meant by rebounding being an exercise that is most beneficial to the body both inside and out. It works all the cells of the body efficiently, and at the same time the exercise puts no unnecessary stress on any part of the body. Rebounding utilizes the natural law of gravity to its full benefit: not only by strengthening the body, but also by doing an exercise which best utilizes the natural inclination of the spine.

The Lymphatic System

Beyond strengthening, rebound exercise also provides the unique experience of cleaning and detoxifying the internal system of the human body. This is done through stimulation of the lymphatic system. To understand this process it is important that we first become familiar with cell function.

The key here is balance. The job of all the cells of the body is to keep the internal environment of the human body in a state of homeostasis. In other words, in a condition of constancy and proper maintenance. How do our 75 trillion cells perform this function? There is a reciprocal relationship between the individual cells as well as between the cells and the fluid around them. For example, when communities of cells which make up specific organs maintain a state of homeostasis, they in turn contribute to the homeostatic condition of the fluid which bathes all the cells of the body—the extracellular fluid. Conversely, so long as homeostatic conditions are maintained within this extracellular fluid, the communities of cells which comprise organs will be positively affected. In this way, all cells both contribute and benefit by maintaining a homeostatic internal environment within the body. Without the proper functioning of this internal environment a person will become sick, and with escalation, this imbalance in the system can lead to death.[5]

The human body is about 75% fluid.[6] Approximately two-thirds of this fluid exists within the cells themselves, and is called intracellular fluid. The remaining third comprises the fluid that exists outside the cells and acts to bathe the cells and carry nutrients from the blood to them. This fluid is referred to by three different names: extracellular fluid, interstitial fluid, or more commonly, lymph fluid. No matter which name one gives to this fluid, it is important to realize that its composition is simple water.[7] This fluid will from here on be referred to as lymph fluid. The importance of the lymph fluid within the human body cannot be under estimated. We must keep in mind that the human body contains three times more lymph fluid than it does blood.[8]

The flow of lymph fluid is the means by which the cells receive the nutrients, hormones, ions, and minerals to ensure they maintain themselves in a state of homeostasis. The lymph fluid is also the passageway by which the cells expel their unwanted material such as carbon dioxide, toxins, and metabolic waste.[9] It is important to note that the flow of lymph provides both the means for the cells to receive their nutrients as well as the means by which cells can expel their waste. As I move along, it is essential to bear in mind that for the flow of lymph to function properly it must literally work as a two-way passage. No matter how many nutrients the cell is able to receive via the lymph fluid, if the means for expulsion of toxins via the lymph fluid is not available, the body will go into a state of profound distress.

Dr. Arthur C. Guyton, renown expert on the lymphatic system, says the following:

> The lymphatic system represents an accessory route by which fluids can flow from the interstitial spaces into the blood. And, most important of all, the lymphatics can carry proteins and large particulate matter away from the tissue spaces, neither of which can be removed by absorption directly into the blood capillary. We shall see that this removal of proteins from the interstitial spaces is an absolutely essential function, without which we would die within about 24 hours.[10]

It is the lymphatic system which removes waste products from the cells that are toxic. The lymphatic system is sometimes referred to as the secondary circulatory system, let us see why this is the case.

The "Secondary Circulatory System"

Our circulatory system is a system of veins and arteries which carry essential nutrients to our organs (made up by communities of cells) via the blood. The metabolic waste must be carried away from the cells, and this is done via the lymphatic ducts. But unlike the primary circulatory system, the lymphatic system does not have its own pump. Whereas the heart functions to pump the blood throughout the body so proper circulation and nutrient distribution can occur throughout, the lymphatic system has no such central pump to propel the toxin-filled lymph fluid away from the cells.[11]

The troubling question is that if there is no specific lymphatic pump within the human body, then how are waste products from the cells propelled away? This is where the relationship between the properly functioning lymphatic system and the practice of rebound exercise is made ultimately clear. Without an internal pump to involuntarily initiate lymph flow, the onus is on the movement of the body. Lymph flow is stimulated by a body in motion, i.e. muscle contraction experienced through physical work, it is stimulated by gravitational opposition, and finally, it is stimulated by internally massaging the lymph duct valves.[12] Rebound exercise is the only exercise which provides all three properties necessary to maintain and increase lymph flow.

A sedentary body will always remain in a certain level of toxicity because waste cannot be effectively pulled away from the cells. Health, which means a maintenance of homeostatic conditions within the body, requires that the body move enough to ensure lymph flow. "Living cells and organs, when continually supplied with proper nutrients and oxygen, will thrive only so long as toxic waste substances are concurrently removed and regularly excreted from the body. This is the main job of the lymphatic system."[13]

The reason I call rebounding a full body exercise which works inside and out is indicative of the fact that I see its function as an internal lymphatic pump as essential. Understanding the lymphatic system is a means by which I have come to fully understand and appreciate one of the most essential functions of rebound exercise. Rebound exercise is excellent for the mind and body, I have established this. But to now uncover how rebounding works to cleanse and detoxify the internal systems of the human body is truly excit-

59

ing. It affords us the opportunity to appreciate how this exercise beyond being fun, efficient, and invigorating, is also one which provides an internal cleansing.

This is exactly what I mean when I call *URBAN REBOUND-ING* the exercise for the new millennium. At this juncture of human development most of us have come to understand the connection between the inner and the outer, and the body and the mind. Rebound exercise is a means by which you can simultaneously uplift your spirit, strengthen your body and its aerobic capacity, while at the same time helping your internal lymphatic system to properly do its job of keeping you clean and free of toxins.

As I discussed in the outset of this book, our modern need for scheduled exercise is reflective of the culture we inhabit. Between the machine age and the information age, we have come to spend more time in a sedentary state than ever before in human history. We do not walk to transport ourselves, we drive a car. We no longer work in the fields to earn our daily bread, we now work sitting for long hours in front of a computer screen. We sit in front of the television and the internet to entertain ourselves and gather information. We are a sedentary culture with a true need for exercise. The idea that the flow of lymph fluid away from the cells would be such a pressing issue, might come as a surprise to our ancestors of two hundred years ago. Lymph fluid movement is stimulated and enhanced by body movement, and everything about an agrarian culture involved body movement. The very survival of this culture depended on effective body movement capable of sustaining work. What the cultures of old did not know, but that we must appreciate, is that movement actually sustains the homeostasis of our internal systems. Movement was such an integral part of the cultures of old, and the ignorance of its internal importance did not jeopardize the health of those cultures.

Rebounding: Stimulation for a Sedentary Culture

On the other hand, for our culture, a sedentary culture, ignorance of the importance of movement to our internal workings can cause us grave damage over time. Like so many other things, progress gives and it takes away. Technological progress gives us conveniences that would be unimaginable to previous cultures, but it also has taken away the means by which we naturally kept ourselves in shape and kept our lymph fluid flowing freely and consistently. We must take responsibility for the consequences of this progress, and on an internal cellular level this means finding alternative ways to generate lymph flow to ensure a healthy internal system. There is no better means for this project than the practice of a steady regimen of rebound exercise.

As early as 1941, the mysteries of the lymphatic system were being explored. Cecil Kent Drinker, M.D. and Joseph Mendel Yoffey, M.D., explain in their book titled *Lymphatics, Lymph, and Lymphoid Tissue*, published by Harvard University Press, that "[N]ormal activity of a part is a potent factor in promoting lymph flow in its immediate environment." And that "[It] is obvious that with uniform activity lymph flow becomes remarkably constant."[14] Almost sixty years ago, "the effects of voluntary muscular activity,"[15] were under consideration by these top research physicians. What these doctors did not have at their disposal was the knowledge of rebound exercise. It is rebound exercise which can catalyze and promote the very effects they were looking for as a means to maintain appropriate lymph flow. The steady motion of rhythmically jumping up and down on the rebounder produces the sense of constancy and balance which the body so desperately demands in order to secure its optimum function.

Doctors Drinker and Yoffey also cite massage as a viable means of invigorating lymph flow. "...[M]assage in the direction of lymph flow is preeminently the best artificial measure for moving extravascular fluid into lymphatics, and for moving lymph onward toward the bloodstream."[16] Rebound exercise has often been referred to as a sort of internal massage. I mention massage here in order to stress the internal power of rebound exercise. The jumping motion on the soft surface of the rebounder is, in a sense, a means of simultaneously not only exercising, but also stimulating conditions that mirror the internal effects of massage. Drinker and Yoffey did not know of the resource for improved lymphatic flow that occurs while rebounding, but they did know of the effects of massage on lymphatic flow. I see a direct relationship between massage and rebound exercise, and therefore, the effects these pioneering physicians noted in lymph flow regarding massage, would also apply today with regard to rebound exercise.

The unique situation of the lymphatic system not having an internal pump such as the heart to move lymph fluid along is the core reason why rebound exercise has the direct relationship with lymph flow that it does. "Instead, lymphatics depend on the contraction of muscles, passive movement of parts of the body, compression of tissue from the outside, and gravity to move the fluids filled with waste to their main garbage dumps in the left and right subclavian veins."[17] Again, this is an area where preventive medicine becomes such an easy task. Think for a minute about the history of human longevity in Eastern cultures like India and China. To what can you attribute this good health and long life? Not to the medical field, most of the communities of note in Eastern cultures where longevity reigns are completely removed from access to modern medicine. The commonality I see is movement—namely yoga in India and Tai Chi Chuan in China. These exercises reflect an ancient wisdom employed to promote not only spiritual well being, but also physical wellness. They are a means of utilizing the natural construct of the body to activate healing within itself.

Consider the balance, coordination, and gravitational opposition necessary to effectively practice either yoga or Tai Chi Chuan. Preventive medicine in the East is thousands of years ahead of us here in the West. In the East, the body is viewed as a system which survives best when it is in balance—or, as I have been saying, when it is in a condition of homeostasis. Whether I am using the medical term of lymphatic flow or the Taoist term of keeping yin and yang in balance, the intentions are the same—to keep the body whole and in harmony. The difference in the East, is that they have considered how such a balance is possible. They have established a tradition of movement which is thousands of years old, a tradition of movement which is as practical today as it was a thousand years ago. We learn a bit slower in the West, and we also have a tendency to need to intellectually understand the internal science of things, before we put them into practice. Going back to our friend Descartes, and that old mind and body split, we tend to forget that our bodies also communicate to us, and that a rational choice would be to listen to the truth our bodies tell us. But we need our minds to confirm that, yes, in fact our bodies do know what they are talking about. Eastern tradition has trusted the relationship between body and mind and therefore has not needed "to prove" the effectiveness of Tai Chi Chuan or Yoga; they have simply felt and experienced its countless physical and spiritual benefits.

We know from our experience that people rebound because it feels good. They have fun doing it and not only get into the best shape of their lives, but have a sense of getting well from the inside out. We here in the West are getting better at listening to our bodies and overcoming the disadvantage of not trusting our physical experience. But nevertheless, our need to rest assured in the "certainty" of scientific study as opposed to the truth of our own bodies, makes the explaining of rebounding's effects on lymphatic flow necessary. For those of you who are bored by this and are more inclined to appreciate the internal science of rebounding intuitively through the practice of it, I of course support this and believe that your practice will tell you more than scientific facts ever could. On the other hand, if you find these explanations interesting and it gives you the encouragement to engage in and sustain a rebound exercise program, then this chapter has done its job favorably.

Therapeutic Rebounding

5

The benefits of rebound exercise exceed the bounds of traditional approaches to fitness. Rebounding is such an effective full body exercise that I feel it imperative that it be utilized as a therapeutic tool while it is also used by thousands as a means of engaging in the finest aerobic and anaerobic work out available. Though the phenomenon of *URBAN REBOUNDING* was born in the group fitness setting, this does not mean that a specialized program of *URBAN REBOUNDING* cannot be tailored specifically for the elderly, the infirm, the wheelchair-bound person, the child, the child with specific learning disabilities, the person with vision problems, the person suffering from bladder trouble, as well as the person suffering from osteoporosis. All persons can benefit from this exercise, so long as it is used according to their specific needs. Let us see how this works.

Rebounding with the Elderly

Before using the Rebounder, I couldn't walk—I literally shuffled and stumbled my way along. Now, I can walk! My body feels lighter. My skin used to be pale and sallow, now it's a rosy pink. Since more blood now gets to my brain, my memory is improving every day.

— James R. Heald[1]

James is not alone in his improvements made on the rebounder. Rebounding is the perfect exercise activity for elderly people for several reasons. The first and most obvious reason is the efficient use rebounding exercise makes of gravity. Gravity is that force which is always resisting us so long as we live. It literally pulls down on us and over time this has a profound effect on the body. Gravity causes the muscles in the face to droop, the breasts to sag, the stomach to protrude, and for the entire person to actually shrink in size as they age.[2] Gravity pulls all the cells of the body downward and inward to produce these effects which most of us have viewed as simply necessary consequences to growing old.

But with the aid of rebound exercise, this no longer need be the case. The very heart of rebound exercise is its opposition to gravity, the G-force gained on the rebounder actually works to counteract gravity's downward pull. In this way, the aging process can be encountered with a sense of equanimity and confidence. The "inevitable" need not be shrinking, poor posture, and a sagging body—rebound exercise can keep the aged person fit and strong.

Poor circulation is a common problem in the older person. Rebound exercise is the ultimate force to circulate lymph away from the cells so toxic waste products can be excreted by the body. Rebound exercise also aids the body in its blood circulation. This constant movement on the vertical plain greatly aids in relieving problems of constipation, which means being able to evacuate the body's waste without putting unnecessary stress on the digestive tract. This also means that the common problem of hemorrhoids among the elderly can be eliminated through rebound exercise. Given the gravitational effects of rebound exercise combined with the fact that all cells get stronger from the exercise, including cells in the bones, posture in the elderly person is vastly improved through rebounding. Rebounding on a regular basis will literally make the elderly person stand taller and stronger.

One of the most common problems people encounter as they age is a loss of balance and coordination. Elderly people break hips, break their backs, or even die every year due to a loss of balance, which has resulted in taking a serious fall on a hard surface. Rebound exercise is an excellent remedy for this troubling state of affairs. The very principles of rebounding work to improve balance and coordination. The constant up and down motion works to regulate itself into the natural rhythm of the body. The body adjusts to the motions and becomes more adept and stable. If the elderly person cannot balance themselves when they first begin rebounding, they can use a stabilizer bar that easily attaches to the rebound unit. With this stabilizer bar serving the function of the common "walker," the elderly person can comfortably begin a rebound exercise regimen. Holding on to maintain stability and gently jumping with their feet will produce a cumulative effect of enhanced coordination. In no time at all they will feel the ability and confidence to let go of the safety bar and to bounce freely.

This should of course be approached with moderation, and at one's own pace, and under the care of a trained health professional. But most often, the body knows when it is ready to let go and experience its reclaimed balance which the rebounding unit is designed to provide. Correcting this problem of loss of balance in the elderly is a great step on the road to increasing the self-esteem and independence of movement that every individual deserves. Very often for the elderly person the loss of balance has meant their loss of independence. Because falling is such a great risk it has meant they can no longer live on their own, and must be cared for and often must give up their homes, their driving privileges, and the ways of life they have forever known. Rebound exercise is a means to give the independence and freedom of association back to the elderly people who desire it.

Balance is not something that needs to be lost with age; through rebound exercise it can be maintained and therefore independence and youthful vigor can be maintained. Remember my reference to the cultures of the East where longevity thrives. The exercise of note in the East are yoga and Tai Chi Chuan, two exercises that focus on not only internal balance as I mentioned previously, but also external balance. Literally focusing on keeping the body in proper alignment, keeping the posture correct, and the body flexible—rebound exercise attempts to do the same.

The benefit for all people, and particularly the elderly person, is the non-jarring effect of rebound exercise on the muscles and joints. The elderly person need not worry about beginning a rebound exercise program, the muscles and joints will not bruise or be adversely affected. The soft cushioned surface absorbs 87% of the shock of the bounce. Rebounding is something that the elderly person can easily do (particularly with the safety bar or a little help from a friend at first), stay with, and improve upon. A rejuvenation and invigoration of body, mind, and spirit can and will ensue.

Rebounding and the Infirm

Rebounding is the fully body work out which functions to strengthen all the cells of the body while it works to help heal the internal systems of the body. Rebound exercise is a cellular and detoxifying exercise, and for some it is a life-saver, just as much as it is a life-enhancer for the average person.

To understand the dramatic effects that rebound exercise can have on one debilitated by sickness and disease, let us look at the situation of Mrs. Laverne Groff of Stevens, Pennsylvania. In 1989, Mrs. Groff was 28 years old and had already been through and recovered from a life threatening physical ordeal. It all began with one ruptured ovary, which was operated on and partially removed. The operation had complications which led to severe hemorrhaging and a close call on the operating table. Later that year, the remainder of that ovary ruptured and needed to be removed. Less than six months later, the other ovary ruptured, and in emergency surgery, half of that ovary needed to be removed. This left Mrs. Groff with only one half of a functioning ovary. After the third surgery, in the recovery room, her heart stopped and she needed to be resuscitated. After some more tests the doctors found it necessary to go back into Mrs. Groff's body yet a fourth time to perform yet another surgical procedure.[3]

This was the absolute breaking point for Mrs. Groff's body. Her weak system was unable to recover from the shock of having all of these surgeries so close together. She developed a strange muscle condition which made it impossible for her to speak for two months. Mrs. Groff could not feed herself because she could not complete the simple motion of moving her arms up and down, and walking was an impossibility. A 28-year-old woman, once in good health, was now in a state of complete infirmity. Though countless tests were done, no cure for Mrs. Groff's condition was found in the hospital which was so eager to perform her four surgeries.[4]

Mrs. Groff left the hospital, but she and her husband refused to give up on her condition—they simply would not accept this state of infirmity as a condition that needed to be permanent—and I am grateful for the perseverance that their example shows. After trying several alternative remedies, they eventually attended a rebounding seminar given by Dr. C. Samuel West, lymphatic specialist. Dr. West introduced the Groffs to the principles of rebound exercise. Dr. West guided the Groffs in team rebounding, a method by which one person can instigate the therapeutic effects of the exercise in another. Mrs. Groff simply sat in a chair and placed her feet on the rebounder as her husband jumped on it. This simple movement in her legs, which was catalyzed by her husband, slowly allowed Mrs. Groff to regain her strength and mobility. After several weeks of this team effort, Mrs. Groff was rebounding on her own for short periods. After several months of this regimen she was rebounding on her own for much longer periods. She was walking, talking, and feeling a sense of wellness and healing come over her. This progressed on and on, and in time, Mrs. Groff became pregnant and had a healthy child. All of this with half an ovary![5]

We have a miraculous example here of what rebound exercise can do, but I do not feel such things to be a fluke. The exercise works all the cells of the body and internal healing is what is supposed to happen—if a body is sick it has the power to heal itself, rebound exercise simply unlocks that power.

Rebounding with the Wheelchair-Bound

The individual who gets around in a wheelchair can greatly benefit from rebound exercise. The bounce increases blood flow to paralyzed areas, aids in general circulation, cleans out lymph, and provides general all around cellular strength. The method to use is a team effort, what I call "team rebounding."

To exercise the paralyzed legs, the technique is quite simple. The person in the wheelchair wheels themselves up to the rebounder, puts their chair in the locked position, and lifts their legs onto the mat of the rebounder. Their feet should be together and they should sit as upright as possible in the chair. Once they are in position, the team partner would get on the rebounder, straddle the person's feet, and begin to gently bounce. The bouncing motion will provide a full benefit to the wheelchair bound individual who need only sit there and receive the health giving effect to their legs.[6]

For the wheelchair bound individual to gain the full benefit of rebound exercise throughout their upper torso, the exercise is also relatively simple. The individual would be helped into position to be able to sit down on the edge of the rebounder, placing their feet on the floor. This type of exercise should only be done if the individual has full use of their arms. If the arms are in good shape, it is easy for the individual to grab hold of the attached stabilizer bar, and maintain an upright sitting position. Once the person is securely in place and comfortable on the rebounder, the team partner simply steps onto the rebounding mat behind the sitting person and begins to gently bounce. This motion will provide cellular strength, lymphatic cleansing, and an overall sense of well being to the upper part of the body.[7]

If the situation is such where the wheelchair bound person has no use of their arms, then there is yet another method for rebound exercise. The individual would be guided to comfortably lay down on the rebounder, while a pillow is placed behind the edge of the individual, on the skirt of the rebound unit. The team partner then steps onto the rebounder and straddles the body of the person laying on it. A gentle bouncing motion will provide invigoration, cleansing, and strength to the person laying down.[8]

All of these sessions should be approached with caution, safety, and care, and should begin slowly. The initial bouncing need last no longer than 30 seconds, three times a day. Allow the endurance and strength to build as you proceed. This is truly a reciprocal team effort in that not only does the person in a wheelchair benefit from their team member's effort, but the able bodied person also benefits by having the best possible reason for remembering to rebound themselves. Not only will both people become healthier and stronger, but a deeper bond of trust and appreciation is bound to develop between the team. I recommend approaching the exercise together, as something that could benefit both parties. The internal rewards of doing the right thing for others is beyond description. It is these acts of genuine human sharing that give meaning to our lives. Team rebounding, executed as I described, provides the participants with an opportunity to experience not only better health, but also a sense of deeper human connection.

Rebounding for the Child

Physicians and psychologists state again and again the importance of those first six years of life of the child. As I said from the outset, children love to bounce—it comes naturally to them. Rather then tell them to stop jumping up and down on your bed, you can now just tell them to go have fun on the rebounder. Children take to this activity naturally. I say activity, because that is exactly how it should be treated with a child. It should never be explained as an exercise that the child needs to do. Children play games and their imagination knows no limits—utilize and encourage this. Let it be a toy for them, something they can dance to their favorite songs on, express their joy and enthusiasm on, and play games of "pretend" on.

All the while, this fun activity will provide the child with better coordination skills, a stimulation of growth, and improved self-confidence. The activity can begin just as soon as the child learns to walk.[9] An adult should be near in case of spills and falls, but the soft surface of the rebounder makes the activity relatively safe. After a while, when coordination rapidly improves, which it will, the child can rebound on their own. The only caution here is that the child should not go from a high bounce on the rebounder onto the floor. This will cause unnecessary stress on the knees and ankles,

71

which is the exact thing we aim to avoid during rebound exercise. The key here is to make this a fun family activity that everybody does. Make it play, and you will see that the joy your child experiences while rebounding will be contagious to you. Think of it, you can both jump side by side, and is not that what kids fantasize about—to have their parents not tell them to stop jumping around, but instead for the parent to actually jump with them!

Develop the habit of rebounding early for your child and it will be one that continues throughout the later years. The early years of childhood are spent in almost perpetual motion, and the idea of being sedentary is completely foreign. However, in our culture of classroom, television, and internet, as children age they run the risk of mimicking adult culture, and living in a more and more sedentary way. Let rebounding be one of the antidotes against the side effects of the child's world which is becoming more and more surrounded by electronic media. Games on the CD-ROM, videos, and the Internet keep children sitting these days more than ever before. This has resulted in over weight children who lack coordination skills and have very limited attention spans. Allow the activity of rebound exercise to serve as something which can counteract a society whose entertainment options for children tend to engage their minds alone, without their bodies.

It is important for the awareness of the mind-body connection to be developed at a young age. Rebounding engages the body in activity; it can easily be done while watching a video. For children to grow up integrated, whole, and healthy they need to understand the workings of their bodies as well as their minds and imaginations. Rebound exercise is a means by which children can continually stimulate their physical senses, while their mental faculties are bombarded by a culture where electronic media reign.

The Learning Disabled Child

Alfhild Akselsen, Ph.D. is the founder of the Texas Association of Children with Learning Disabilities, the association is located in Austin, Texas. In her over 40 years of experience working with learning disabled children she has found three problems which mark a common denominator in the cases she has worked: "Learning disabled children have extremely poor coordination, balance, and rhythm," notes Akselsen.[10]

Dr. Akselsen began her career as a school psychologist in Norway where it was her responsibility to work with children categorized as learning disabled. She began experimenting, searching for a common thread that would tie together a reasonable hypothesis as to why these children were having problems in their classes. After meeting failure in her search for commonalities, Dr. Akselsen tried a rather basic physical approach. She simply asked one of the children to walk backwards. He could not do the act, falling down after just three steps. Distinguishing left from right was also difficult for the child. After many more physical tests on the children, it became apparent to her that the keys were balance, coordination, and rhythm.[11]

After much trial and error with different exercise programs aimed at improving balance, coordination, and rhythm, Dr. Akselsen finally came upon the use of the rebounding device. Remember the chapter on the history of rebounding and the industry's first manufacturer, Victor Green. After experimenting with the children jumping on something like a wooden springboard, she found out about Victor Green's Tri-Flex plant. She visited the plant, found those first rebounders which resemble what we use today, and she brought them back to use with her learning disabled students. The results that Dr. Akselsen got from working with the students on the rebounders were truly astounding. The experience made her a true believer and the first pioneer of rebound exercise for the learning disabled child.[12] Dr. Akselsen has said:

> Rebounding should start in Nursery school. I see mind/body improvement occur throughout the growth period of the human organism. When I work with a child who has all kinds of coordination problems culminating in learning disabilities it means he or she has not worked with the gross and

fine motor nerve/muscle coordinates. A child should do this from at least first or second grade. I have put rebounding devices in schools around the world. The children have to be given a chance to learn up to their capacities.[13]

Dr. Akselsen has come to understand the principles of the cellular exercise which rebounding provides. She explains her success with children this way:

...[W]hen you are rebounding, you are moving and exercising every brain cell as you are each of the other body cells. Toxic heavy metals are leached out of these brain cells to free up the neurons to work more effectively. Better nourishment has a chance to penetrate the cell walls, too. Furthermore, rebounding has you work from the outside, from the nerve endings toward the brain. That's what I think it does. We don't know for certain, of course, but I can't see the results any other way.[14]

As in other areas of this young exercise, more research needs to be done by the medical community in order to bring a consensus of confirmation as to the properties involved in therapeutic rebounding. Nevertheless, the results do have a tendency to speak for themselves. Another case of rebound exercise having successful results with learning disabled students, comes via a report from a teacher of aphasic students. In the middle of the 1970's, Mrs. Florence M. Franet was a teacher of aphasic (a condition resulting in the loss of ability to speak or comprehend words) students at the Mount Diablo Unified School District in Concord, California. Like so many others of the 1970's, Mrs. Franet bought herself a rebound unit for her own personal use, she had fun doing it and she liked the way it made her feel. She figured she would share it with her students. Transporting the unit back and forth became too much of a chore, yet the students enjoyed it so much that she decided to buy one for the class. In the 1976-1977 school year, Franet used the rebounder on a regular basis in her class for aphasic students. Six students between the ages of eight and nine participated in the activity.[15] Mrs. Franet comments on the progress of one of her students:

At the beginning of the school year Frances could not coordinate her small motor development enough to draw a circle or copy a single letter. She did attempt to write her first name, but one had to know what Frances was attempting in order to read it. Her eye/hand coordination was nill. Her speech was unintelligible. She used only small words and sometimes short phrases.

After one month of using the rebound unit, Frances was bouncing with two feet by herself. Following this, she developed sufficient coordination to run slowly on the rebound unit. In four months, Fran was running and dancing on it. Her language developed along with this. In four month's time you could also read her name when she wrote it. She could draw circles. In six months, she could trace the letters of her last name. In eight months she could copy her last name. In nine months she could write it by herself...Frances's verbal expression developed along with her written and motor expression. She was using simple sentences, gradually extending them into whole paragraphs by the end of these nine months. Her receptive language improved also.[16]

Across the board Mrs. Franet saw improvements like the kind Frances made. Rebounding proved to be a new and exciting way to give these students the help they so desperately needed. In this light, Mrs. Franet reported the following:

All of these students showed growth in their coordination, language skills, health, and attitudes. I had expected to see growth for these students and had worked with aphasic students for five years previously to working with this group. But this group far exceeded expectations. I attribute their additional gains and development and total stimulation to the use of the rebound unit.[17]

We provide you with these two inspiring examples on what can be done with creativity, persistence, and an eclectic approach to health, as a means to begin thinking more seriously about the potential for the rebound device. The results are real and need to be taken into account when considering alternative therapies for any variety of problems involving children with disabilities.

Rebounding for Vision Correction

Like so many other non-traditional approaches to medicine in the West, we do not hear about them too often in the mainstream. Western medicine has a history and philosophical disposition which puts the onus of cure solely on the professional physician. The body has not been viewed as a whole system of interrelated parts that work together to form a cohesive entity, but instead as a variety of disconnected parts that can be treated as isolated cases. I see this when it comes to invasive surgery, I also see it in the way medicines are prescribed. Knowing this, it is not surprising that care for eyes in the West is handled, by the majority, in a similarly disjointed fashion.

There are two kinds of practitioners involved in vision correction of the type which does not require surgery. Surgical procedures are done by an ophthalmologist, but vision correction is undertaken by an Optometrist of two types: the Structural Optometrist or the Developmental Optometrist (Visual Therapist). Most of us have never heard of a Visual Therapist, but are quite familiar with the Optometrist. The traditional Optometrist does not attempt to ameliorate imperfect vision via any sort of therapy for the eye, rather, the Structural Optometrist prescribes corrective lenses.

For a variety of reasons, people may find they have vision problems from the earliest years, and the Structural Optometrist will fit such individuals with the proper prescription for glasses to correct the impairment. The problem is that no measures are taken to improve upon the vision problem, it simply gets worse over time, and as it does new prescriptions are needed. Glasses grow thicker, eye sight grows worse, and production of eye wear increases for the optical industry. In the United States, as of 1989, there were approximately 25,000 practicing Optometrists, and of that 25,000 only approximately 800 engaged in form of visual therapy.[18]

Given this state of affairs, it is no wonder that visual therapy in this country is not well known, however, the Developmental Optometrists that are out there represent a growing and very enthusiastic movement. It was no surprise to me to discover that vision therapists across the nation are using rebound exercise as their main therapy for eye strengthening and vision correction therapy. Noted Vision Therapist and Developmental Optometrist, Theodore S. Kadet, O.D., had the following to say about the use of rebound exercise to improve vision:

Rebounding creates an awareness of using vision as a primary guiding system for movement. The inability to use vision efficiently as a major sentry system to the brain can be a primary cause of learning disabilities in children and adults. I am confirming what other authorities have found before me. Our treatment in optometry of these visual perception dysfunctions help Mother Nature along in the development of vision and vision-auditory interaction systems.[19]

In vision therapy the functions of the eye are not taken as some separate category of function. Vision is taken by Developmental Optometrists as a holistic system capable of healing itself with the proper guidance and instruction. Dr. Kadet further explains this type of visual therapy engaged in while on a rebounder:

We concentrate on such areas as visually guided body movements; hand-eye coordination; visual size, space, form and direction relationships; visual-auditory integration; figure-ground relationships; visualization and memory skills. The rebound device is used to bring about efficient visually guided movement of the entire body. Rebounding aerobics gives magnificent feedback as to what the child did, thus bringing about a rapid awareness as using vision to guide movement.[20]

The idea of coordination, rhythm, and balance, put forth by Dr. Akselsen, as a key to working with learning disabled children, is coming up again here in relation to vision therapy. There is a direct connection to the body's reaction to rebound exercise and how this reaction effects eye stimulation. Developmental Optometrist, Dr. Albert Shankman, of Stamford, Connecticut, explains this phenomenon further:

In rebounding, you have to learn to use your muscles and do it quickly, if you don't learn muscle coordination on the rebounding device, you will face a severe consequence of falling and possibly hurting yourself. Whenever there is a consequence you will learn faster. Rebounding requires that you keep your balance, and you use your eyes for this purpose. By rebounding the same way, using the same exercise positions time after time, you are bound to come to a saturation level where your eyes won't improve anymore. But changing the exercises so as to force yourself into new balancing positions will have the eyes continue their improvement. You get the benefit from rebounding for the sight and mind by relating the objects around you to the space which you are occupying as you jump up and down.[21]

In other words, while rebounding, one focuses on their surroundings as they jump. This exercise helps one establish and improve depth, distance, and other types of visual perception. Developmental Optometrist, Dr. Raymond Gottlieb, of Santa Monica, California, agrees with Dr. Shankman's analysis and adds supporting information with regard to the relationship of vision to rhythm. He states that, "One of the characteristics of people who suffer from insufficient vision is the lack of rhythm. The rebounding device gives rhythm to the brain from the systematic bouncing. This allows the eyes some externally generated rhythm to fall back on and thus become more coordinated."[22]

Besides the connection of rhythmic bouncing, space, and vision coordination, Dr. Gottlieb also stresses the basic therapeutic effects of rebound exercise as a significant cause to visual improvement:

> ...[W]ith the greater circulation stimulated from rebounding, you will have more energy for seeing. There is circulation of the cerebral spinal fluid in the brain, enhanced lymphatic circulation, and better blood circulation. Any toxic circumstances possibly interfering with vision centers will be dissipated.[23]

Vision therapy is yet another avenue where rebound exercise has had a great impact and will hopefully become more widespread.

Rebounding and Bladder Control

More often than not, when a person has a bladder control problem, the last thing they want to do is exercise, because so many exercise programs will only make matters worse. Most problems involving control of the urinary bladder are related to a weakened sphincter muscle. The sphincter on the bladder is an annular (circular in shape) muscle which through opening and closing, controls the flow of urine out of the body. If this muscle is not functioning properly, and for some reason has lost its strength, elasticity, or its proper shape, the results can cause an individual to have a "weak bladder." This could mean a variety of things for an individual. A minimal disturbance can mean simply that the individual needs to make several trips to the bathroom every day because the bladder is such that it can only contain so much liquid at a time. At the other end of the continuum would be an individual whose bladder sphincter has degenerated to such a state that the leakage is constant throughout the day.

The remedy for the former has been to structure one's life so that a bathroom is never far away at any given moment, and this can be quite limiting and a real burden. The remedy for the latter case has been to wear protective garments. Rebounding is an activity which strengthens every cell in the body, including the cells that make up the sphincter muscles of the bladder, as well as the bladder lining. To build strength in the cells takes time, and results might not come right away. But in time, changes in bladder function will be noticeable if a steady program of rebound exercise is followed.[24]

As stated, rebound exercise works muscles as well as the internal organs of the body. A steady program of rebounding will exert a force on the cell walls of the bladder such that it will react by becoming more elastic and durable. In this way, the discipline of rebound exercise can once again lead an individual to not only have a healthier life, but a freer one. Without having to contend with the burden of a weak bladder, one's quality of life will be drastically improved. And that is what rebound exercise is all about—to improve the quality of one's life, no matter what the initial limitations.

Rebounding and Osteoporosis

Osteoporosis is a condition which is caused by a loss in mass of individual bones in the body, which in turn, cause the spaces between bones to grow larger. As a result of this loss in bone mass and strength, osteoporosis causes a bodily condition which is characterized by the bones becoming frail and porous. "Osteo" means bone, and "porosis" means that water is able to pass through. A bone that becomes porous cannot perform its intended function of providing structural shape and support to the body. An "osteocyte" means simply a bone cell, of which there are two types: "Osteoblasts" and "Osteoclasts." The osteoblast is a bone forming cell and the osteoclast is a cell which removes unwanted mineral matter in the bone. "Osteocytes are constantly remodeling the entire skeletal system, depositing more mineral in the bone tissue where bones are under the greatest amount of stress and removing minerals from the bone with the least amount of stress. Therefore, bones become stronger when stimulated by exercise and weaker with little or no exercise."[25] The condition known as Osteoporosis takes over the body when the balance of bone cell activity is dominated by osteoclasts, an agent which removes bone mass rather than rebuilds it.

If you recall from chapter 2, I mentioned the NASA study done on astronauts that found that in conditions of a zero-gravity (weightless) environment, astronauts lost an average of 15% of their bone mass in a 14 day period. The remedy to rebuild was rebound exercise. The combined force on the vertical plane of acceleration, deceleration, and gravity produced the sensation in the body of a triple gravitational force. This increased pressure made all the cells of the body react by becoming stronger. This includes an increase in osteoblastic activity.

Rebound exercise makes for stronger bones, the same way it does muscles and internal organs. Rebound exercise should of course always be thought of and used as a preventive measure against such conditions as osteoporosis. However, if this prevention was not available, the person suffering from osteoporosis can still find great relief by using rebound exercise. If an individual cannot stand or maintain balance due to their condition, they can use the team rebounding techniques described earlier in this chapter. These team rebounding techniques will cause the bones to become stronger, and in time the individual will hopefully be rebounding, as well as doing many other activities, independently.

Rebounding: A Better Way to Better Health

Rebounding is a tool by which individuals of all kinds can provide themselves with the means for therapeutic healing. There is no magic involved in this, it is simple physics and biology which explain the principles of how rebound exercise stimulates cellular strength and internal cleansing. All that is needed to begin a program of therapeutic rebounding is the right equipment, and a willingness to trust the fact that you can be an active participant in your own healing.[26]

URBAN REBOUNDING:
An Exercise for the New Millennium

6

Why do I call *URBAN REBOUNDING* an exercise for the new millennium? Is this just another means of exploiting the use of the millennium for commercial means? After all, M&M candy calls themselves the candy of the new millennium because MM is the Roman numeral for 2000. In this way, throughout our media-laden culture, the use and significance of the coming millennium begins to become trivialized. This tendency toward triviality in our culture has no place here. I do not mean to say that the coming millennium holds within it the keys to unlock the secrets of the universe, and at the approach of 12 midnight on December 31, 1999 our lives will be changed forever. I do not mean that at all. The millennium is not a magic number or a magic date. As somebody once said, "millenniums may be happening every other minute, it depends on which point in time you started counting from." No, I do not believe in the magic of dates in and of themselves, I am more apt to agree with Shakespeare when he had Hamlet say "...for there is nothing either good or bad but thinking makes it so."

Indeed, it is our thinking which makes it so! What do we think about the new millennium is the question. A date is a date, but how we interpret that date is up to us.

An Opportunity for Change

I choose to interpret it as a time for potential change and growth to occur for the individual who willingly embraces the new millennium with a new and open mind. An individual not bound by the dualities of body and mind of the past age, but rather an individual open to the possibility for true connection between mind and body in this new millennium. Such changes will not happen in and of themselves through some magic, we must make it so. And how do

83

we make it so? How do we make the new millennium into a meaningful event for our lives?

I would argue that the means to make it so are to embrace it as a real opportunity for change. An opportunity to build a richer and stronger relationship between the body and the mind. Allowing the body and mind to live in sync with each other will create a sense of well being and health that everyone deserves to have and needs to have. One of the ways I see this health coming about is through rebound exercise. All of the elements to combine the best of Western scientific analysis and Eastern medicine are present within the framework of rebound exercise. *URBAN REBOUNDING* is a means by which the elements already present in rebounding are married together with elements of Eastern philosophy. I have written throughout about the evolution of rebound exercise, *URBAN REBOUNDING* marks a point of integration. The goal of *URBAN REBOUNDING* is to encourage a way of living that integrates the body and mind in such a way where people can live as wholly and fully as possible. Health is a life-long process, it is not a singular event. If anything, the system of *URBAN REBOUNDING* means to embrace the new millennium as a means of beginning a new process towards living a more integrated life.

A Personal Note

To understand how I discovered rebounding and how I came upon this method of integration called *URBAN REBOUNDING*, it is necessary for you to know a bit of my own history. My background is in the martial arts. I have been a teacher of the specialized art of Okinawan GoJu-Ryu for fifteen years. I have also trained in a specialized Chinese breathing and movement system known as Qi-Gong. In my youth I trained almost exclusively in what is known as the "hard arts." Quick and fast movements (Go), hard punches and kicks with a focus on combat. As I got older, I began to understand more and more about the philosophy of the martial arts and came to slowly and steadily appreciate what is known as the "soft arts": Slow rhythmic movement (Ju) with a focus on perfection of form and a harnessing of internal "chi " or "Qi". The word means energy or life force, and the soft arts focus on the preservation and efficient utilization of this energy. Qi-Gong focuses on a steady rhythmic method of deep breathing to increase awareness and strength. The Ju style of Okinawan GoJu-Ryu Karate focuses on achieving harmony via balancing the body through dance-like subtle movement.

I came upon rebounding after I seriously injured my knee while practicing the hard form of martial arts. Three different doctors recommended that I have surgery to repair the damage, but I knew that the kind of surgery they recommended would never allow me the full healing I would need to get back into martial training. So I opted for a different approach. I went to see a doctor of Chinese medicine and he gave me a specially made mixture of topical herbs for my knee. It was the worst smelling concoction I have ever known, but it did provide me pain relief.

In the absence of my training, and having not yet discovered either Qi-Gong or the soft side (Ju) of Okinawan Karate, I was searching for a means to rehabilitate my knee. Through a long trail of speaking with different people involved in the alternative medicine field I was lead to Albert E. Carter's 1977 book, *The Miracles of Rebound Exercise*. I was skeptical, but I saw the soft surface as a means to practice my Katas (martial art forms) without having to subject my knee to the hard wood floor of the dojo (martial arts studio). I ordered a rebounder and began to practice my martial art postures on its soft surface. Over time, my knee improved and I went back to training in the dojo without ever having the knee surgery.

When I first began training on the rebounder, I thought it would only be a temporary measure, something to do until my knee regained its full strength. But even after my knee was back to normal, I continued to rebound. There was something about the smooth rhythmic motion that calmed and invigorated my body simultaneously. I felt a heightened awareness and level of energy

85

from rebound exercise. In time, I went on to discover Qi-Gong and the soft side of Okinawan Karate, and I incorporated them into my training, but I never abandoned my daily routine of rebounding.

Rebound exercise was no longer something I used for rehabilitation but had become an integral part of my training. At first I did not understand my connection to rebounding. It seemed odd to need a modern piece of equipment to supplement refined systems such as Okinawan Goju Karate and Qi-Gong that were thousands of years old. But the more I used the rebounder the better I came to understand the relationship of rebounding to these soft arts I was practicing. The experience of weightlessness encountered through the rhythmic bounce of the rebounder produced an internal feeling of being supported. The bounce produced a sense of surrender, a sense of letting go yet remaining fully connected and present to the experience. This is exactly the notion that the soft arts aim to encourage. Rebounding was helping me to be in touch with this experience of surrender working together with profound concentration.

As my training progressed, things began to formally culminate in the martial art which always remained a part of me, Okinawan GoJu-Ryu. I supplemented my training with Qi-Gong, and rebounding, but never gave up the art which first started me on my path. In 1985 I came upon a master teacher, Mr. Kaw Loon "Kayo" Ong, and it was he who truly opened up the inner core of GoJu Ryu for me. "Ryu" means simply the way of. "Go" means hard and "Ju" means soft. "Kayo" showed me that in my practice of Okinawan GoJu-Ryu, I was taught to focus simply on the "Go"-"Ryu"—the way of the hard. I practiced rock hard focused punches, kicks, and quick movements. But "Kayo" explained that in doing this I had only been exposed to half the art. The other half, the "Ju"-"Ryu," means the way of the soft. Refined, flowing, fluid motions grounded in the center of one's being. Hard and soft together, a harmony and balance of the two, and the more I trained this way the more all the other arts became subsumed in Okinawan Go-Ju-Ryu.

86

I trained in a small Dojo in Chinatown, New York, where Mr. Ong ran classes in the old Okinawan style. A class cost only $3.00 per session, and if one could not afford that price they could train free—this is the traditional way. I trained without a belt, so as to stress that the focus of learning was to always be on the means and never on the ends. The fact that I was a black belt was to be forgotten when I entered his class, I was to enter the dojo with "beginner's mind." A mind open and free to explore and experiment with new forms, a mind not encumbered by the burden of pride which makes one complacent and afraid of failure. Failure was important in Mr. Ong's class, it was a tool to understand limitation, and to understand how to succeed. Success was never judged however, not from the outside. I was taught to work inward, to feel the path of striving as a personal journey one where only I could determine my own degree of success.

My practice of rebounding grew also as I discovered this profound integration between hard and soft in the martial arts. I practiced my postures on the rebounder with a refined technique, knowing the softness of the rebound surface would always support me. Rebounding fed my martial arts training and my martial arts training fed rebounding. There was something about the circular shape of the rebounder and its stationary position that made me a better martial artist. The rebounder reinforced the need to keep my center of gravity low and it helped to structurally define control of movement. By control, I mean simply that on the rebounder, no matter how complicated the kata (martial art movement), it had to be performed within the parameters of this 28 inch diameter space. The only place to go was up on the vertical plane, not out on the horizontal plane. The rebounder gave me a refined control which I never would have imagined possible. To be forced to contain a movement in a defined space allows the sensation of the movement to focus down and inward, and in this, I was able to experience the integration of hard and soft—the *way* of the hard and soft—as a true reality.

I continued to study Okinawan GoJu-Ryu in all its perplexity and ultimate simplicity, this apparent paradox of hard and soft became clearer and clearer over time, so long as I approached every session with "beginner's mind" and remained open. I also continued practicing my forms on the rebounder as well as developing variations of them to attain maximum benefit from the G-Force gain while rebounding.

This process went on for a solid twelve years, and in time I came to develop a systemized program of training on the rebounder. The key to the forms in GoJu-Ryu is the structure of the stance—the necessity of achieving optimum balance. The posture has been likened to the structure of a tree. The feet must be firmly rooted, experiencing a downward pull that keeps them planted in the earth. No matter how much movement, no matter how complex the movements, the simplicity remains that the feet always come back to this rooted position. But in life there is wind, rain, and snow, and the tree must adapt. If the tree were only hard and firm all the way through it would never survive. Though the trunk must remain centered and planted, the limbs must be prepared to flow with the way of nature. The limbs must be flexible enough to bend as snow gathers on them, bend but not break. The limbs must be pliable enough to sway with the wind, rather than hold fast against it and risk snapping in half. And when the season changes and it time to fall, the leaves must go their own way and the limbs must be prepared to let them go. New growth must be allowed to develop through periods of apparent dormancy. New buds must be given time to flower and finally mature to leaf, only so the whole process can be repeated again and again in a cycle of rhythmic balance. And all this while the trunk consistently stays firmly planted, providing an unshakable foundation for change and growth to occur. Though the trunk grows old, each season is new, each bud, each flower, each leaf, has its own individual presence and new birth to share with its guardian, the tree, which provides their ultimate support.

GoJu-Ryu is this way. The bottom part of the body must be a firm root, planted into the core of the earth. No matter what positions develop, one must always remain in tune with this ultimate center. Movements are anchored, fluidity is tethered in such a way that the body can always be confident of its own balance and harmony. This balance in form and stance connects to the mind over time, and the psyche too finds its root. New movement, new ideas burst forth in arrays of color and form, yet they are always balanced by the truth of the roots of constancy.

Rebounding tested my balance and coordination so much because now I had a soft surface to work against. Working on this pliable surface brought the nature of balance into sharp focus for me. Whereas before, I always thought of the earth as a constant which exerted no force of its own upon me, the rebounder taught me through practice to think differently. Rebounding brought me a heightened sense of awareness with regard to the ground underneath my feet. In GoJu-Ryu, I was always taught to jump off the balls of my feet and when I came down to come back into the center of my stance by "jumping through the earth." I never truly understood this phrase, not for a long time, and it was only on the rebounder that the meaning made itself clear. "Jumping through the earth," meant to land with a certain intention, an intention which brought you back to complete rootedness. Because the rebound surface is soft and pliable, you can actually "jump through it," you feel it give way on every bounce. The ground under your feet literally gives way as you jump through it with the balls of your feet.

This sensation of jumping through the mat produces the profound feeling of establishing roots in an earth which bends to accept your presence. In other words, the rebounder makes it clear that balance is essential and that the earth responds openly when you strive to achieve balance. This may sound strange, but when it is practically applied and experienced, it is ultimately natural. The soft surface of the rebounder enforces the necessity of balance. The key here is intention—deep focus on staying on the balls of the feet and literally "jumping through the surface," this action creates a refinement in technique, balance, and posture which was astounding to me.

URBAN REBOUNDING Is Born

The joy, exhilaration, and fitness I experienced through rebounding was a true gift. I had trouble understanding why rebound exercise was not everywhere. Why more people would not want to benefit from it, whether they were martial artists or not. In doing some research and checking into what kind of rebound instruction was available, I soon came to understand the nature of the problem.

There was a lack of focus on technique and intentional method when it came to rebound exercise. The jump itself had an unfocused quality and with that the technique can easily become sloppy. The katas or forms, as they exist in the system of GoJu-Ryu, are meant to bring a deep integration of intent upon execution to the body and the mind. It is this focused intent geared toward integration of body and mind that is the foundation of the *URBAN REBOUNDING* training method.

In this way participants are guided not to race and not to flounder, but to intentionally focus on the shape, form, and extension of every jump. To receive maximum benefit of the exercise the mind must cooperate with the flow that the body attempts to execute. For this to happen properly, the mind must not be distracted by extraneous thoughts, it must be a willing participant with the body. This state of focused integration is achieved through balance, rhythm, breath control, and intention. By establishing proper rhythm, breathing follows, proper breathing brings correct intention, and proper intention achieves optimum balance. This is the way it works, and balance, or the homeostasis, is the ultimate goal which is meant to be attained and maintained throughout.

Meditation is often thought of in terms of sitting in the lotus

90

position or a kneeling position, remaining still, and breathing. But this sitting meditation is but one kind of mind/body work. There is also walking meditation, in which the touch of each step is focused, and clear rhythm of breath and movement is established. This is a common practice among Zen practitioners. What I aim to establish on the rebounder is a similar principle. It is a bouncing meditation, in which rhythm, breath, intention, and balance are cultivated. Each individual can find the focus to help them achieve their goals of healing, rejuvenation, and optimum function. *URBAN REBOUNDING* makes full use of the science of rebounding, and what it adds is a philosophy and practical method.

When I say that the exercise of *URBAN REBOUNDING* brings great joy to those who do it, I do not mean this in a superficial way. Once individuals begin to re-discover, or perhaps find for the first time, the natural rhythm of their bodies and they begin to witness their own new found sense of well being, they connect with the inner joy that was always buried there waiting to be unlocked.

After twelve years of practice and experiment with developing a methodology of rebound exercise, I decided it was time to share it with others. Originally I thought I might simply share it with fellow martial artists in the GoJu-Ryu system, but in time I came to see that would not be enough. The simplicity and the structure of the exercise was such that I knew I could teach it to anyone, regardless of their fitness level, so long as they approached things with an open mind. To test my system I started out in a small health club in New York City. I wanted to see if my GoJu-Ryu teaching style coupled with my own personal philosophy would transfer to the health club format. My hopes were not high, I figured if I could reach a few people, that would be enough.

In my wildest dreams I never could have predicted the success of this initial class. People were more open to my system than I ever would have guessed. Word spread and my classes had long waiting lists. The success and enthusiasm of that first class gave me the confidence in my teaching to branch out. The major health club chain

91

of New York soon picked up my class and it became so popular that people were only able to get in by reservation. As things grew I began to train aerobic instructors around the country in the *URBAN REBOUNDING* system. In the period of a few short years *URBAN REBOUNDING* has become a national and an international phenomenon. To what do I attribute this success? Two things. One is the underlying philosophy which undergirds the methodology and practice of the exercise. I will go into this in greater depth as the chapter continues. But secondly, and most importantly, it is the participants whose energy, determination, and good will make this exercise what it is.

Why "Urban"?

I have often been asked why I call the system *URBAN REBOUNDING*. The rebounding part is clear enough, but why the "urban" part? Urban means simply, something which constitutes a city. Do I call it *URBAN REBOUNDING* because the exercise started in New York City? No, it was not that simple a choice. If that were the case I could have very well called it CITY REBOUNDING, which I did not and would not. Urban is directly related to the word urbane, which connotes a state of refinement or polish. The two words are intimately related, though we often forget that in today's world. The exercise system I developed is indeed urbane, because of its practiced refinement and focus on exquisite detail. This is one part of why the word urban is so fitting for it. But more than that, I mean to trace back to the original meaning and purpose of a city.

If you recall the first chapter, I began my discussion of exercise by talking about the Greeks and the great city of Athens. This first great site of urbanity where democracy was born, drama was powerful, philosophy was profound, and athletics were valued as a means for perfection of the mind and the body. Athens was our first great city in the West, our first true urban center which was indeed urbane. Cultivation of the body and the mind was valued—it was a place where Pericles, Euripides, Socrates, Plato,

Aristotle, and Alcibiades all contemplated the meaning of existence. An Urban center was a place for people to come together so they can make a better life, one of shared responsibility and community.

URBAN REBOUNDING is a very small way in which I try to create an atmosphere for an enriched sense of community within which people can flower. Not a city of separate apartments with everyone walled off inside their own cubicle, and living blind to the plight of their neighbor, but a true urban (urbane) community of individuals. A group of people who come together to invigorate their body and their mind, and paramount to this is that they do this together. The rebounder is an individual personal unit, much like an apartment, it is one's own space. But put those rebounders side by side and across a room and at once we have a community, a sort of city without walls. Individuals engaged with their own body, mind, and space, but at the same time engaged with a group that is working together as a larger unit.

The apartment is no longer sealed off, the individual is working next to their neighbor though they fully inhabit their own space. I do not know how to define this quality of the class in definitive terms, it is a bit mysterious to me still. But something seems to occur in which not only do people become more open to themselves, but they become more open to others. One who feels the joy within themselves seems to be able to sense it in another, and almost involuntarily, connections between people are made and sustained. There is no magic here, just people being their natural selves—I have seen it in the martial arts all my life. So in short, this is where the term *URBAN REBOUNDING* comes from. The "urban" represents the refinement of the exercise and the community it builds within the people who practice it. I cannot stress this enough, that one of the two reasons that this exercise system is so successful is that the people who practice it are open to themselves and to each other and such an openness of spirit brings joy.

The Way of *URBAN REBOUNDING*

The other reason for the success of *URBAN REBOUNDING* is the philosophical school which underlies it. Behind GoJu-Ryu, the hard and soft, is the yin and yang, or as it is known in China, the Pa-Kwa. The balance of the extremes, the hard and soft, the still and the fluid. The idea comes from the Chinese philosophy known as Taoism. In Chinese, Tao means "the way," just as "Ryu" means "the way" in Okinawan. To follow the Tao is to follow the "middle path," the way of balance and harmony. The oldest and most influential Taoist philosophical text is called the *Tao Te Ching*, which means simply "*The Way of Life*," by Lao-Tzu. To best understand the nature of where the philosophical underpinnings of *URBAN REBOUNDING* come from it is important to see it in its relationship to the *Tao Te Ching*. Follow along as I go through a bit of "*The Way of Life*" to make clear what is meant by the way of *URBAN REBOUNDING*.

> *Gravity is the root of grace,*
> *The mainstay of all speed.*
> *A traveler of true means, whatever the day's pace,*
> *Remembers the provision-van*
> *And, however fine prospect be offered, is a man*
> *With a calm head.*[1]

Let me take this a sentence at a time so it can be explained completely. "Gravity is the root of all grace,/ The mainstay of all speed." Here I relate to the literal as well as the figurative meaning of this phrase. It is the law of gravity which is at the heart of rebound exercise. This natural law that we all live with is utilized to our true benefit. It is this gravity which keeps us rooted to the earth, but it is also the temporary triumph of gravity which produces such subtle moments of grace. Think of Michael Jordan, Mikhail Barishnikov, or the late great Isadora Duncan—a body in flight is a masterpiece made to be captured forever in stone by the likes of Michelangelo and Rodin. An artist wants to sculpt such flight so it can be preserved there for eternity, a reminder that the human being holds within itself the ability to overcome any limitation. In URBAN REBOUNDING we understand our rootedness to the earth—our firm stance, but at the same time, we experience fluidity, temporary flight, and in that there is grace. For me "gravity is the mainstay of all speed," in that it is gravity which determines the acceleration and deceleration of our movements. The natural law is our guide, and we operate on its plane, on its terms, and in so doing, we remain in harmony with our nature.

"A traveler of true means, whatever the day's pace, remembers the provision-van/ And, however fine prospect be offered, is a man / With calm head." Health is a process not an event. In this way, I view someone entering an URBAN REBOUNDING class, no matter their level, as a traveler on a journey to holistic healing and true health. For me the provision-van represents the ultimate staple of life—the self-possession of an integrated body and spirit. In URBAN REBOUNDING we always want to remember the ultimate goal of whole health and an integrated body and mind, and we do not want to get lost or bogged down with other "prospects." Whether that "prospect" involves too much self-criticism, too much competition among students, or too much focus on outward reward or outward appearance, we aim to stay intentionally focused on our "provision-van" of whole health. In doing so, this is the means by which one maintains a "calm head," from which follows a calm body, which brings about a balanced and homeostatic integrated relationship between body and mind—and this is our ultimate goal.

> *There is no need to run outside*
> *For better seeing,*
> *Nor to peer from a window. Rather abide*
> *At the center of your being;*
> *For the more you leave it, the less you learn.*
> *Search your heart and see*
> *If he is wise who takes each turn:*
> *The way to do is to be.*[2]

On the rebounder we exercise our body and mind but never leave the center of ourselves. Gravity grounds us to return to the center of our being; to feel our center and experience our natural untainted nature that abides beneath the surface of defense and insecurity. To be comfortable with one's body is to begin the journey of finding comfort in one's mind and finding the peace which makes life rich. We move on the rebounder, but only up and down, our bodies are rooted—we cannot run from ourselves. We must look at our centers, at our forms, see where we are out of balance and see where we are not. The rebounder gives us a chance to stay close to ourselves and to reside within a process of rhythmic moving meditation. What can be discovered there in that space of the center of the being is a secret that each individual discovers for themselves. Once that secret is known, the body and mind seem to work together without much effort, they seem simply to know each other and truly, "to do is to be." To do the forms of *URBAN REBOUNDING*, to do them with the full intention of the body and the mind is to forget the day's problems and to truly be in the moment. And when we live in the moment we can live wholly and become ourselves, because truly, the eternal is the now.

> *Man, born tender and yielding,*
> *Stiffens and hardens in death.*
> *All living growth is pliant,*
> *Until death transfixes it.*
> *Thus men who have hardened are 'kin of death'*
> *And men who stay gentle are 'kin of life.'*
> *Thus a hard-hearted army is doomed to lose.*
> *A tree hard-fleshed is cut down:*
> *Down goes the tough and big,*
> *Up comes the tender sprig.*[3]

This saying is abundantly clear and it represents the heart of Taoist thought. The way of life is a way of gentleness, flexibility— be like the water not the rock. The water erodes the rock, but this is only done in time and with a constant flow. In *URBAN*

REBOUNDING one is taught to appreciate what I call "flow." To flow in the moment of movement, to stay so intently within that flow that all else fades away and life is suddenly simple. The gentleness of the rebound mat will never injure your body, your knees, your ankles, no matter how forcefully you bounce. In this way we have a double gentleness, our own flow and the cushion of landing on a surface which yields to our weight. To be alive is to adapt to life's changes, to be flexible and always willing to grow.

In *URBAN REBOUNDING* one must constantly adapt to new forms, new music, new rhythm. To adapt, one must be free enough to move without fear of losing balance. How do we do this? How do we do one movement with full intention and then change to another movement and maintain full intention? To do this, we must flow; we must remain in harmony despite the changes in pace that occur. This is the way of life, constant change to which we must adapt and thrive. *URBAN REBOUNDING* is no different, it mirrors life's way. It is a means to test your ability to maintain focus and proper intention while adapting to change. The body must maintain flow so the mind can grow in freedom and concentration. In *URBAN REBOUNDING* we constantly practice the art of transition. We aim to master the skill of maintaining focus throughout periods of change. This is the struggle in life, to remain in harmony as we are in the midst of change. To be able to do this is to be able to live well. One never ultimately masters this but is always in the process of striving. In *URBAN REBOUNDING* we focus on mastering such things, and the hope is that some of what we experience in the safety of a class transfers out into the difficulty and complexity of the world.

By understanding the philosophy of *URBAN REBOUNDING* as well as the biology and the physics of it, my hope is that you get the fullest picture that you can, whether you have yet experienced the workout for yourself or not. In the hopes of broadening the scope a bit further, I would now like to share some of the more recent media reports about *URBAN REBOUNDING,* as well as some of the personal experiences of a few *URBAN REBOUNDING* students.

The Media Celebrates *URBAN REBOUNDING*

Elana Zeide highlighted *URBAN REBOUNDING* in the October, 1998 issue of *New York* magazine. "...*URBAN REBOUNDING* classes, which combine traditional aerobics moves with specialized jumps, all performed on one's personal trampoline. The workouts offer cardiovascular benefits without the hazards of high impact exercise." The story was soon picked up by several national magazines, including *American Health*, *Fitness*, and *Fit*.

The February 1999 article in *Fitness* said: "*URBAN REBOUNDING*, a 60-minute low-impact workout on a mini trampoline, burns fat, increases agility and boasts a huge fun factor." *Fitness* magazine did a follow-up piece the next month in March which said:

> What's so unusual about wind sprints, boxing punches, jumping jacks and swim strokes? Everything—when you do them on a mini-trampoline [rebounder]! The *URBAN REBOUNDING* trend we reported on last month has taken off. Now Crunch health clubs across the country are offering it as a 45-minute group fitness class led by JB Berns and his disciples. Rebounding allows you to work harder—and for longer—than most workouts because your energy isn't being used to absorb the shock of a hard surface...Anyone can do it; it's an especially good alternative for people who need to avoid high-impact workouts like running. The calorie burn is comparable to jogging, but with no stress to the joints of the lower body—and rebounding is a lot more fun.

Writer Megan McMorris did a feature story titled simply, "*URBAN REBOUNDING*," in the April edition of *Fit* magazine.

> As we begin jumping, it becomes clear what the class is about. We jog, turn, twist, sprint, kick and box...Although I catch on quickly, the great thing about trampolining

[rebounding] is there's always room for improvement. And the class provides that elusive tough-yet-low-impact quality...the class's popularity does qualify it as the next Spinning, with one exception: It's fun!

In late April Julie Sevrens did a feature length story titled "Rebounding, a 70's Fitness Craze, Is Making a Comeback." The story first ran in the "San Jose Mercury News," and was later picked up by several papers across the nation. In the article, Sevrens quoted Richard Cotton, the spokesman for the American Council on Exercise as calling the comeback of rebounding "a resurrection." Cotton goes on to say: "It's a low-impact activity, and it does enhance coordination and balance." The article continues to highlight *URBAN REBOUNDING*:

...URBAN REBOUNDING is quite different from the rebounding of years past. If there is one reason why rebounding should stick around a while longer, it's the physical benefits it has to offer, fitness experts believe. The activity works a number of muscle groups, including the hamstrings, quadriceps, and glutes, while providing a solid aerobic workout.

URBAN REBOUNDING was also featured quite frequently over the past six months on the medium of television. Barbara Walters' hit talk show, which airs on ABC, "The View," spotlighted *URBAN REBOUNDING* in its "Body & Soul" segment in February of 1999. JB Berns jumped with co-host Meredith Viera as she touted the "exercise that truly gets you high!" Later that month the *URBAN REBOUNDING* technique was featured as the "Fit Tip" on the FOX network's news segment "Fox on Health."

Physician for NBC local news in New York City, Dr. Ian Smith, did a special report on *URBAN REBOUNDING* in which he highlighted the health benefits of the exercise. "...by fighting gravity and increasing your heart-rate you can get an aerobic workout as challenging as running, but it's on a softer surface."

Dr. Smith emphasized *URBAN REBOUNDING*'s therapeutic

properties: "While it may be new in fitness centers, it's old in the world of rehabilitation." In explaining the mechanics of how *URBAN REBOUNDING* works, Dr. Smith had this to say: "...the exerciser bounces so hard at the height of the bounce you experience weightlessness, similar to what an astronaut experiences while floating in space."

"Now by constantly working against gravity, cellular strength is built. Some also believe that the pumping helps to cleanse the body. It pulls waste from the cells and replaces it with oxygen and nutrition from the bloodstream." Dr. Smith also discussed *URBAN REBOUNDING*'s benefits to the bones and joints when he said that rebounding, "reduces the amount of stress and impact on the joints, but at the same time it allows you to have still an intense cardio-vascular workout."

Dr. Ian Smith also focused on the diversity of movements in the *URBAN REBOUNDING* system: "There is a definite challenge on your coordination as you work muscles that otherwise wouldn't be exercised on a regular surface." In summing up his report, Dr. Smith concluded: "The importance of aerobic workouts in preventing heart disease, diabetes, obesity, and other medical syndromes has been well documented. Working out on the trampoline [rebounder] is a great way to still get that cardio-vascular challenge, without too much stress on the joints and ligaments."

In March of 1999, *URBAN REBOUNDING* was a featured segment on the FOX network's popular national broadcast, "The Donny and Marie Show." Donny and Marie kicked and jumped into health as the national audience got a lesson in the science of rebounding.

Monica Pellegrini, reporter for New York's Channel 9 news show, "Sports Team," did a special report on *URBAN REBOUNDING*. Ms. Pellegrini had this to say: "This exercise [*URBAN REBOUNDING*] uses the trampoline [rebounder] to produce a sense of weightlessness similar to what astronauts feel in space, but here on earth the benefits can be not just better aerobic conditioning, but a healthier body." In discussing the health benefits, Pelligrini reported: "...[T]he constant non-impact bouncing can help increase the body's oxygen supply as well as aiding in detoxification of the body." After taking a class herself, Pellegrini could not help but be tickled by the sense of joy one gets from *URBAN REBOUNDING*: "Once you get going though, it's fun, it's cross-training, and you feel a little bit like a kid!"

Julie Golden did a "Get Fit" spot on *URBAN REBOUNDING* for ABC's local morning show "Good Day New York." Excited by the innovative movements of *URBAN REBOUNDING*, she had this to report: "A lot of people get in a routine of they get on the treadmill or they get on the bike and it just seems a little monotonous after a while, this kind of spices it up a bit..."

The CBS network's national Saturday morning news program with Hattie Kauffman, featured *URBAN REBOUNDING* in the segment, "Cutting Edge workout." Kauffman introduced the segment this way: "We're always on the look-out for new workouts that can add some spice or variety to your fitness program...it's *URBAN REBOUNDING*!" Kauffman went on to introduce fitness expert, Bonnie Kay, who reported on her experiences with *URBAN REBOUNDING*. Kay had this to add: "*URBAN REBOUNDING* is designed to increase cardio-vascular fitness but without the jarring of doing high impact moves on a hardwood floor. In fact, rebounding has been a rehabilitation tool in physical therapy settings for years because it's gentle on your bones and joints but it does challenge your coordination."

The Lifetime Network featured *URBAN REBOUNDING* in April of 1999 in their "Lifetime Original" segment. It was introduced with fire; "It's called *URBAN REBOUNDING*, and talk about hot, it could be the workout of your life...Those who've tried it say it's a blast." The story went on to break through the rhetoric and get to the heart of the matter: "*URBAN REBOUNDING* is a total body workout and it burns as many calories as jogging without stressing the joints." The "Lifetime Original" also noted the therapeutic effects of the exercise: "To get the most bang out of this bounce you've got to have technique...the G-force acts like an internal massage to oxygenate and detoxify the body."

On the morning of April 27, 1999, New York's most popular talk-radio station, 1010-WINS, did a special report on *URBAN REBOUNDING*. Radio reporter Alice Stockton-Rossini praised *URBAN REBOUNDING* as being both "easy on the knees" and helping to "bring joy back into exercise." On May 10, 1999, the "Sally Jesse Raphael Show" featured *URBAN REBOUNDING*, in its segment on health on the woman's body. The action of rebounding has a particular effect in slimming the legs and eliminating varicose veins, a topic which was of great interest to the show's predominantly female audience.

Students Celebrate *URBAN REBOUNDING*

It is one thing to hear from journalists who have experienced *URBAN REBOUNDING*, but I thought it might also be helpful to hear from some of *URBAN REBOUNDING'S* veteran students.

• Julie Kim, a 25-year-old who participates at least three times a week in an *URBAN REBOUNDING* class, says that, "this is the most dedicated I've ever been to any sort of exercise regimen—probably because it's the most fun I've ever had! I love the classes, the instruction is phenomenal...really motivating." Kim also notes some of the results, after just *URBAN REBOUNDING* for five months, "As a runner, since rebounding, I can run longer, with more energy, without the aches and pains that I used to have. I've never been in such good condition...my body is leaner, more toned, and stronger." Cindy Rosenshein, age 30, agrees, "I love rebounding! I feel like Superman when I'm finished! I've also never been so entertained and engaged while working out. I was doing Spinning for a year, but that got boring, with rebounding I'm not only not bored but I'm in better shape than ever. I feel every inch of my body being worked. My stomach, my arms, my legs...it's just the best."

- Nancy Hirsch, age 34, has been an Aerobics instructor for sixteen years. She came to *URBAN REBOUNDING* looking for a challenge and for reinvigoration, and she has found it. "This is a dynamite aerobic workout, my whole body just feels cleaner, between the G-force and the oxygenation, I really feel it working as I'm doing it." Hirsch also notes her state of mind while in the class, "my mind feels clearer, the repetitiveness of the jumping feels very natural to my body." Ms. Hirsch became such a believer in the power of *URBAN REBOUNDING*, that she herself became a certified instructor just two months ago, and now teaches in New York City.

- Blake Mays, a 32 year-old male living in New York City, has been an Aerobics instructor for ten years. He is also a trampolinist and a gymnast. Discovering *URBAN REBOUNDING* was a sort of revelation for Blake, a way of bringing together many of his greatest joys regarding fitness and recreation. Blake says that *URBAN REBOUNDING* is "a lot of fun...I feel incredible while doing it, and I'm never sore when I'm done, but don't get me wrong, it is the most challenging cardio workout I've ever done." Coming from a gymnast and a ten year veteran instructor of Step Aerobics, I was surprised to hear how challenging Mr. Mays felt *URBAN REBOUNDING* to be. He states, "it's easy on your knees, I never feel pain the way I do after teaching STEP [Aerobics], but I do always feel challenged and never bored." Blake attributes the results of his leaner shape and strengthened abdominal muscles to the gravitational pull of the rebounder. Since first trying *URBAN REBOUNDING* six months ago, he still attends class twice a week, and has now begun to incorporate *URBAN REBOUNDING* techniques with his own clients which he personally trains.

- Lisa Levin, age 30, attends an *URBAN REBOUNDING* class as many mornings a week as she can. She says the 7:30 am class she attends is "all energy" and that she leaves class feeling

103

"totally energized, never sore" and like "the entire hour just flew by." As a runner, Lisa said that rebounding has made her faster, and that as an avid tennis player, Lisa claims rebounding has made her serve stronger. In terms of results, Ms. Levin tells us, "it is a full body workout which sculpts, firms, and strongly defines my whole body — I'm just glad I found *URBAN REBOUNDING*."

- Andre Saroba, a 32-year-old male of New York City says, "*URBAN REBOUNDING* is the only workout I've found to make my 'love-handles' disappear. I achieved the results I wanted in no time, I keep doing it because it's so much fun and I've never felt better." Andre feels this to be a great alternative and break from other workouts he has tried. "The principle of using the G-force, and that weightlessness feeling is like nothing else I've ever experienced."

- Terry Hirbert, age 29, has been *URBAN REBOUNDING* since September 1998 and she manages to maintain a rigorous schedule of at least three times a week. "I see a difference in my energy level on the whole—my body is leaner and my legs are stronger." After class, Terry says she feels "amazing, not tired at all, I'm completely energized and ready for anything...I love this class!" Terry said that *URBAN REBOUNDING*, beside being physically great for her, has also been a tremendous in-class experience. "Step Aerobics always made me feel like I was in someone else's way, always bumping into people, with *URBAN REBOUNDING* you have your own personal space on the rebounder, yet you get the full motivational benefits of a class setting—it's great!"

- Lois Choi, a thirty-something New York City resident, has been teaching Aerobics for seven years. "*URBAN REBOUNDING* is the best workout I've ever gotten. You work really hard—it's challenging, yet accessible." When I asked her to what reason does she attributes the success of

URBAN REBOUNDING, she answered: "*URBAN RE BOUNDING* is a lot more applied. In the past, so many Aerobics classes have been misguided, this class [*URBAN REBOUNDING*] applies principles of conditioning, physiology, and strength training in a very enlightened way." Describing her feeling about the exercise, Ms. Choi said, "it's invigorating in a certain way, it is hard to explain, but it is a unique feeling being on the rebounder—stimulating to the entire body." Ms. Choi teaches upwards of 20 aerobic classes per week, I asked her how she finds time for *URBAN RE-BOUNDING*, and why she does it in addition to all her classes. "Simple," she replied, "the results are amazing, I've never seen these kinds of results, not ever—and for your entire body, I was surprised by it, and just want to keep staying with it."

- Jennifer Doctorovich, age 31, has been *URBAN REBOUND-ING* consistently three times a week for seven months. She used to have knee problems from Step Aerobics, but no more. "The low-impact of *URBAN REBOUNDING* is exactly what I was looking for, after doing all that Step [Aerobics] I needed this. I have a leaner look throughout my whole body, the cellulite is gone, and better still, my circulation is better." Improved circulation is of course just one of the many therapeutic benefits of rebounding. Besides the physical benefits, Ms. Doctorovich also describes the psychological benefits of the class: "It's that one hour of the day to leave all the stress at the door. I'm able to completely focus my mind and body on what I'm doing in the moment. As a dancer, it reminds me of a dance class in that way. I feel exhilarated when I'm rebounding, and when it's over there is a heightened awareness within my whole body." Aimee Tumaneng, age 24, agreed with Doctorovich when she told us, "it is therapeutic in that way, like yoga, you just feel this calm when you're done."

- Ms. Tumaneng particularly enjoys what she calls "the martial arts twist" of *URBAN REBOUNDING*. "The movements can get more refined over time, but they are not hard to learn at first, that's what I like about it. Step Aerobics just kept getting more and more complicated—this is simple yet always challenging." Because of its complications, Aimee gave up Aerobics and returned to using the treadmill and stationary bike for a while—until she discovered *URBAN REBOUNDING*. "The machines get so boring after a while, and you're so isolated, *URBAN REBOUNDING* is exactly what I was looking for, I'm so glad I found it."

- Lauren Brenner, a 26-year-old Wall Street Trader and competitive tennis player, has been doing *URBAN REBOUNDING* for the past year. "I just got addicted to the class," she said. "I do the workout four times a week because it makes my life better—it's as simple as that!" Lauren had reconstructive surgery on her bladder some years ago, and has had a weak bladder for as long as she can remember. "*URBAN REBOUNDING* has definitely strengthened my bladder, I never felt this good. I also know it's been better for my immune system. So long as I'm rebounding, I don't get sick." Ms. Brenner calls herself "a true believer" and recommends the class to all her friends. Lauren added a final note that not only is *URBAN REBOUNDING* wonderful for her body, but for her mind, it serves to completely unwind and relax her after a hard day's work.

URBAN REBOUNDING: For Life

In some cases, the results from *URBAN REBOUNDING* are quite dramatic. Understandably, many of these inspirational individuals do not want their name used. One such individual is a 43-year-old male who has been *URBAN REBOUNDING* twice a week for nine months. I will call him simply "A." *URBAN REBOUNDING* is an integral part of A.'s rehabilitation program. A. is HIV-positive, a diabetic, suffers from chronic pancreatitis, and he suffered a heart attack three years ago. Three years ago he was hospitalized for six months and was unable to get out of bed or eat solid food for five of those six months. Still unable to work, A. has made incredible strides over the last two years, and particularly over the last nine months. A. told us, "I have to do a cardio workout for my rehabilitation and I love this class, it's fun and a great workout. My mind is always focused on what I'm doing and it never feels forced. I feel a real change in my physical body since I started rebounding."

A.'s progress is a tribute to his own hard work and dedication, and it is wonderful to provide a class in which he can improve so rapidly. A. is *URBAN REBOUNDING* in a regular class, but under the direction of his physician. In cases of extreme physical ailments, I always recommend seeking a physician's advice before *URBAN REBOUNDING.* I share these stories with you so that they might serve to inspire and uplift you as you continue or make a new beginning on your own journey to full and whole health.

The *URBAN REBOUNDING* Workout 7

In this chapter, my aim is to show and describe the standard *URBAN REBOUNDING* workout in all its detail. I will describe the workout format, discuss proper equipment selection, explain the different kinds of bounces to be used on a rebounder, discuss the nature of the *URBAN REBOUNDING* technique, and finally, I will provide a breakdown of all components of the individual movements of the workout.

The Workout

The standard *URBAN REBOUNDING* workout format follows a prescribed, pre-choreographed pattern, which ensures consistency, full participation, and a system in which skills can be progressively built upon. I begin with a warm up on the floor, off of the rebounder. This warm up is similar to the kind done in a low/high impact aerobics class. I concentrate on warming up the lower half of the body first, and then the upper half. I do this to music at 130 beats per minute for a total of four minutes. Once the body begins to warm we get onto the rebounder and warm up for four minutes to 130 beats per minute of music. In this warm up we want participants to make a smooth transition from warming up on the floor to warming on the rebounder. In this phase, it is important to become comfortable with the movements you will doing over the course of the entire workout. The body needs to adjust to the surface of the rebounder, and the warm up phase marks that period of adjustment.

Once the body is warm and comfortable on the rebounder, we go into our first aerobic phase, which lasts 26 minutes and is done to the music of 132 beats per minute. In this first aerobic phase, many of the movements mimic the movements of high/low impact aerobics. The movements of the upper body often mirror the movements made while working out with free weights. It should be noted that all of the aerobic movements can be done with sand weights in hand. This is called resistance rebounding, and is done on the intermediate level.

After this aerobics section, we move on to sports-specific exercises, such as running, sprinting, and skiing. All movements are coordination movements geared to enhance balance and agility. This segment is done for four minutes to the music of 145 beats per minute. What follows is a four minute segment done without music, called strength bounces. The strength bounce section is done according to specific instructor cues. Strength bounces represent short explosive movements done for power. Use of higher G-force ratio is employed during this segment which lasts for a total of four minutes. Following the strength bounces the next eight minutes of workout is split between a cool down on the rebounder and then a cool down off the rebounder. The cool down is the same as the warm up, to ensure consistency and balance. The cool down is done to the music of 130 beats per minute.

The last phase of the *URBAN REBOUNDING* workout is done with no music at all. Like the strength bounce phase, it is dependent on instructor command. This five minute section is the abdominal workout, and is done completely on the rebounder. At this phase, abdominal bounces or seated bounces are performed on the rebounder with the body in a ninety degree position . The participant is to maintain a concentrated focus upon squeezing the lower and upper abdominal muscles together in order to achieve maximum benefit. The physics of the body against the rebounder produces the most efficient abdominal workout in existence. To review this entire 55 minute *URBAN REBOUNDING* standard workout, it looks like this:

1. Warm-up on floor: 4 minutes at 130 bpm

2. Warm-up on rebounder: 4 minutes at 130 bpm

3. Aerobics I: 26 minutes at 133 bpm

4. Sports: 4 minutes at 145 bpm

5. Strength Bounces: 4 minutes; no music

6. Cool-down on rebounder: 4 minutes at 130 bpm

7. Cool-down on floor: 4 minutes at 130 bpm

8. Abdominals: 5 minutes; no music

Equipment Selection

The standard circular URBAN REBOUNDER should be employed to ensure maximum efficiency and safety. A well supported cross-training sneaker is ideal for this exercise. I do not recommend rebounding barefoot. Women should wear a well made support bra and men should be sure to wear an athletic supporter.

The Bounces

1. The basic exercises on the rebounder are gentle bounces where the feet do not leave the mat. They are called BASIC BOUNCES because of the internal cleansing effect such movements initiate to the lymphatic system. These simple bounces can be done by anyone and are what is used exclusively for therapeutic rebounding. This is the movement which serves the function of acting as the body's own lymphatic pump, by gently pushing lymph out of the body. The BASIC BOUNCE is what is known as the transition move in *URBAN REBOUNDING*. It is the posture from which we move through as we go from one type of exercise to another, and it is also from this posture that all cues are given. The BASIC BOUNCE is used during warm-up and cool-down periods.

2. After warming up for several minutes with the BASIC BOUNCES, one is ready for the AEROBIC BOUNCES. In the center of the rebounder start the technique. It is not necessary for the participant to wait for the rebounder to bounce to move on to the next movement. AEROBIC BOUNCES are employed for the aerobic segments of the workout. The feet do leave the mat, and the jumps are higher and faster.

3. The STRENGTH BOUNCES are the bounces which pro-

111

vide all the cells of the body with an experience of maximum G-Force. It is a bounce characterized by higher and more explosive movements than all other bounces. STRENGTH BOUNCES are employed for the sports-specific as well as strength bounce segments of the *URBAN REBOUNDING* workout.

4. ABDOMINAL BOUNCES are performed while sitting on the rebounder with the body at a 90 degree angle. The feet are either both on the floor, or one is flexed and extended outward during the bounce. For an individual who has become exceptionally proficient at this technique they may want to try this with both feet off the ground. To perform the technique this way, one sits in the middle of the rebounder, lifts their legs to a 45 degree angle while their back is also at a 45 degree angle. This will form the individual's body in the shape of a V. Without touching the ground, one uses the propulsion of one's arms to keep the bounce going. This type of bounce is excellent for the abdominals and should only be attempted by the advanced student.

To review, the four types of bounces to be utilized in the *URBAN REBOUNDING* system are:

1. BASIC BOUNCES

2. AEROBIC BOUNCES

3. STRENGTH BOUNCES

4. ABDOMINAL BOUNCES[1]

The *URBAN REBOUNDING* Technique

The *URBAN REBOUNDING* technique is the key to the entire workout. I return here to the metaphor of the tree. Throughout the workout it is imperative to retain a strong center of focus in the lower part of the body. This technique is established early on in the workout and applied as it proceeds. First comes the proper stance, and all else follows from there. Like the tree, the trunk must be firmly rooted if the tree is to bear fruit. To achieve this the center of gravity is kept low, the body leans forward 8-10 degrees, and the knees are slightly bent. One remains on the balls of their feet at all times, alert, focused, and prepared for movement. All jumps are controlled and focused, the participant will generally not leave the mat more than a vertical distance of six inches. Form, quickness, coordination, and concentration are stressed, the body should be relaxed but prepared. On all hand movements the hands are held in a fist to signify intention of purpose. A martial arts stance as well as focused intentional movement structure is the heart of the *URBAN REBOUNDING* technique. It is the carefully executed precision of this technique which creates an atmosphere of methodical rhythmic refinement. Lastly, but most importantly, it is a technique of joy designed to create an open pathway for the body to experience the full benefit of its movements.

Below, you will find the actual structure of a standard *URBAN REBOUNDING* class. Following this break down will be a series of photos of JB Berns properly demonstrating all the specified movements of the *URBAN REBOUNDING* workout. These photos will be accompanied by detailed explanations of the movement pictured.

URBAN REBOUNDING CLASS STRUCTURE

WARM-UP ON THE FLOOR
(each movement eight times except for stretches)

1. March narrow then wide
2. 'Tap out' on balls of feet
3. Hamstring curls
4. Side to side
5. March, tapping rebounder
6. Groin stretch
7. Leg stretch, lunge, heel stretch
8. Push-ups, heel stretches

WARM-UP ON THE REBOUNDER
(each movement eight times except for stretches)

1. Basic bounce
2. 'Tap-out' on balls of feet
3. Hamstring curls
4. Side to side
5. Basic bounce
6. Jog in place
7. Jog delay
8. Jog in place
9. Repeat (2-4)
10. Basic Bounce

AEROBIC SEGMENT
(each movement eight times)

1. Small jump, big jump (feet only; hands on waist)
2. Small jump, big jump (hands, tricep/bicep movement)
3. Knee raises (hands, shoulder flex movement)
4. *URBAN REBOUNDING* jumping jacks
5. Twisting hips (hands parallel) 45 degree twist
6. 180 degree twist (hands parallel)
7. Double foot bounce (hands, military press)
8. Forward jump (hands, lateral raise)
9. Upright-row
10. Knees to Chest

SPORTS SEGMENT

1. Basic bounce

2. Jog in place (24 seconds)

3. Four sets of sprints (16 seconds)

4. Jog in place (24 seconds)

5. Basic bounce

STRENGTH BOUNCE SEGMENT
(each movement eight times)

1. Vertical jump

2. Twist 180 degrees

3. Power jump

COOL DOWN ON REBOUNDER
Same as warm-up on rebounder

COOL DOWN ON FLOOR
Same as warm-up on floor.

ABDOMINALS ON REBOUNDER

1. Sit on rebounder and bounce alternating left leg and right leg extensions (eight times)

2. Two sets of eight crunches

3. Repeat step 1

This is the standard 55-minute *URBAN REBOUNDING* workout. What follows is a pictorial breakdown of the movements.

A Photographic Breakdown of *URBAN REBOUNDING* Equipment and Movements

This is the official *URBAN REBOUNDER*. It has a 28-inch jumping surface. One can be ordered by calling 1-(888) JB-BERNS.

This movement marks the transition from the warm-up on the floor to the warm-up done on the rebounder. This is the key position for the *URBAN REBOUNDING* technique. It is from this stance where instructor cues are given. The hands are on the hips, the eyes focus straight ahead, the knees are slightly bent, the body leans forward 8-10 degrees, and we stand on the balls of our feet. The center of gravity is kept low with concentrated intention on the body's center. As in Okinawan GoJu-Ryu, it is the stance from which all other things come. A poor stance will mean a poor technique. The proper stance must be practiced and focused upon to ensure a successful workout.

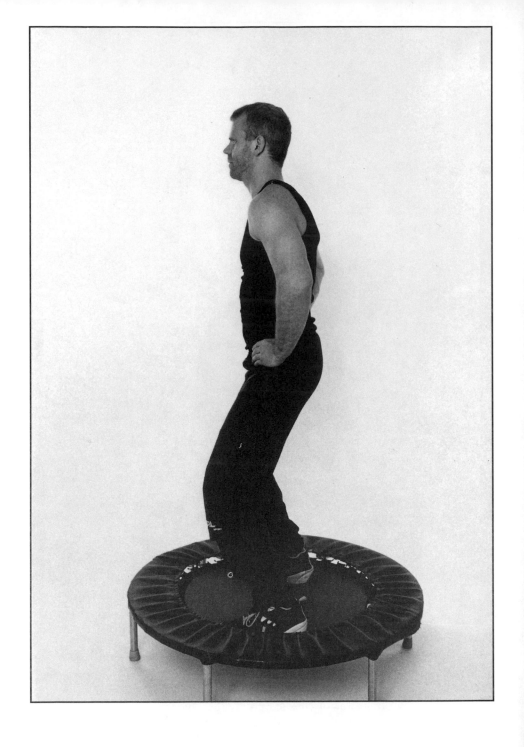

This is the lateral view of the *URBAN REBOUNDING* stance. Note the bending of the knees and the straightness of the back—this is key.

118

Now warming-up on the rebounder, we perform a 'tap-out' of the feet while on the rebounder as we simultaneously do a lateral raise with our arms. We stay on the balls of our feet, the fists stay closed to mark our intent, and the eyes focus straight ahead.

This is the hamstring curl done on the rebounder. Both arms simultaneously perform the reverse tricep curl as this is done.

120

We move from side to side on the rebounder in fluid rhythmic motion. Arms are in front and are extended slightly. Intent is important here, they eyes should remained focused on a particular spot in the room.

121

We jog in place on the rebounder. We lock our upper and lower abdominal muscles, the knees come forward (parallel to waist) and the arms perform a pumping motion. Once the jog is comfortably established in this position, we move into the jog-delay. The jog-delay requires us to hold our position on one leg for a two second count as we jog. This is done to test, improve, and execute balance and coordination techniques.

Here we move into our BASIC BOUNCE. It is from this position that all instructional cues are given. Besides being a bounce for internal health, it serves as our transition move as we go from one segment to another. Remember to keep the back straight, the knees bent, and the center of gravity low. As we move into the aerobic section the music is increased to 132 beats per minute.

This marks the beginning of our aerobic section. This move is known as "Straddle-A." This small jump is done with the feet together, on the balls of the feet, and leaning forward 8-10 degrees. This feet together movement represents one half of the move. A reverse tricep curl is applied during this move. This exercise isolates the muscles of the calves, quadriceps, hamstrings, buttocks, and abdominals.

This movement is known as "Straddle-B." It is the counterpart move done with "Straddle-A." From the feet together position of "Straddle-A," the feet jump out wide as the arms simultaneously come in a bicep curl. This movement is done in a smooth controlled rhythm. Together, "Straddle-A" and "Straddle-B" work to from a cohesive unit of refined movement.

This movement is known as the Lateral Knee Lift. One knee raises as the arms swing upward to create a shoulder fly. This is done alternatively between knees. We always stay on the balls of our feet and intently push-off the rebounder as we move. The lateral knee raise focuses on working the calves, quadriceps, hamstrings, buttocks, abdominals, and shoulders.

126

This is our standard *URBAN REBOUNDING* jumping jack. We stay on the balls of our feet, the back is straight, and the hands make a fist to signal intent of the movement. Stance is essential here and this move provides a good opportunity to check the structure and rhythm of one's technique. Again, this movement will work the calves, quadriceps, hamstrings, buttocks, and abdominals.

This movement is known as the 45 Degree Twist. While standing in the center of the rebounder, we bounce so that the hips and legs turn to the left, while the chest and shoulders turn to the right. We then come back through with the hips and legs turning to the right, and the chest and shoulders turning to the left. The feet should always remain close together, the back straight, and the focus is straight ahead.

This movement is known as the 180 Degree Spin. While standing in the center of the rebounder, with the legs shoulder width apart and slightly bent, we jump 180 degrees around then back forward. The arms help propel the jump as the shoulders remain parallel. In this move the calves, quadriceps, hamstrings, buttocks, abdominals, and shoulders are worked.

This movement is known as the Military Press. With the feet together, the knees together and slightly bent, the arms perform a military shoulder press. We jump in the same spot on the rebounder as this movement is performed. Maintaining focus on that spot along with the eyes focused straight ahead is most important as this move works to sustain balance and concentration. Again, the fists are closed to signify proper intention. This move works the calves, quadriceps, hamstrings, buttocks, abdominals, and shoulders.

This movement is known as the Forward Jump. We jump forward on the rebounder and then backward as the arms simultaneously perform a lateral shoulder raise. The feet and knees are together, and the knees are slightly bent while the back remains straight. Eyes are focused straight ahead, and hands are in fist to signify intent. Again, the muscles to be worked on this move will be the calves, quadriceps, hamstrings, buttocks, abdominals, and shoulders.

This movement is known as the Upright-Row. The lower part of the body is performing a simple Lateral-Knee Raise, while the upper part of the body concentrates on a shoulder isolation move. Notice the fists are closed to signify intent and the upper body maintains a focused center. Again, this exercise strengthens the calves, quadriceps, hamstrings, buttocks, abdominals, and shoulders.

This movement is known as the Forward Knee Lift. Each knee will alternate being raised to a parallel level with the waist. As this is done, the hands come down across the raised knee as if the hands holds a board of wood which they aim to break over the raised knee. The move focuses on calves, quadriceps, buttocks, hamstrings, abdominals, chest, and shoulders.

133

This is the transition BASIC BOUNCE move to signify our transition from the aerobics segment of the workout to the sports-specific segment of the workout. The stance is checked and the center of the body defined.

134

This Rebounding Jog is similar to the one done during the warm-up, except that the pace is faster. The music moves up from the 133 beats per minute of the aerobics (1) segment to 145 beats per minute in this sports-specific segment. Four intervals of 24 second sprints are also employed at this time. This is done opposite a 16 second jog interval. In addition to this movement working the buttocks, hamstrings, quadriceps, arms, and abdominals, it also serves as an optimum pitch workout for the cardiovascular system.

This movement is known as the Slalom. It is a movement which mimics the act of skiing down a mountain. We jump from side to side with the feet together, and the hands are kept out at waist level as though they are gripping ski poles. The back remains straight, the knees bent, and we are always on the balls of our feet. All the motion is in the hips, the upper body should remain completely focused and still. This gives an intense workout to all muscles in the lower torso, particularly the hips. This movement provides excellent means for one to gain perfect balance.

We return to the rebound jog and then move into an extended jog-delay with a rapid pumping motion of the arms. The aim here, at this pace, is to truly test balance and coordination. The exercise will concentrate on the buttocks, hamstrings, abdominals, quadriceps, and arms.

Just before this movement, the instructor uses the standard BASIC BOUNCE transition move to signal the transition of the sports-specific phase into the Strength bounce phase. Strength bounces are done without music, they are performed based upon instructor commands. The first Strength bounce move is a Vertical Jump. The legs are bent, the hands are held open and up, for balance, and we look straight ahead. We perform an explosive jump off the rebounder. Remember, it is in this section where we strive to attain maximum G-force.

138

This movement is known as the Strength bounce 180 Degree Spin. The jump is higher than in the aerobic(1) section. The arms and shoulders are parallel and the movement is done in short explosive bursts.

There are no additional pictures for the cool down, because they are the exact same as the warm-up on rebounder and warm-up on floor. Going through the cool down routine with proper intention will ensure consistency, familiarity, balance, and increased flexibility. When you have finished the cool down on the rebounder, and cool down on the floor sections, you can move on to the Abdominal section.

140

There is no music accompanying the abdominal section of the workout. It is done based upon instructional cues. With the body at a 90 degree angle, sit down on the rebounder and bounce. The back is straight, the eyes look straight ahead, and we focus on squeezing the lower and upper abdominals together.

This is a frontal view of the same posture.

The upper torso remains in the 90 degree posture. Bounces are now done with one leg straight out, with the foot in flexed position. This is alternated between legs.

This is a frontal view of the straight leg, flexed foot posture.

There is no accompanying photo, but the last abdominal exercise on the rebounder is a standard abdominal crunch movement. This is done with the buttocks on the center of the rebounder. This concludes our standard *URBAN REBOUNDING* workout.

Through careful execution of the of *URBAN REBOUNDING* workout, your strength, agility, stamina, and confidence will increase with each passing day. Stay focused on the process and not the end result. Remember, health is a process, not an event. The results will take care of themselves if you are vigilant about practicing the means to those results.

Pay attention to your body and to what it needs. Only you know what you can handle right now. If a twenty-two minute aerobic section is too long for you in the beginning, then do it for only ten minutes, or even five. The point is to do it. Simply begin! Work at a pace that is comfortable for you, monitor your progress and watch yourself improve. Never push yourself to the point of exhaustion or to the point where your movements become sloppy. Keep in mind the technique of *URBAN REBOUNDING*. It should increase bodily balance, harmony, and a general sense of well being. This is an exercise that is good for you, and it should feel food while you are doing it. The moments spent on the rebounder should be a joy, if it becomes a chore it is time to re-evaluate the attitude you are taking toward the exercise.

The knowledge and the tools are at your command, it now up to you to trust your ability and to begin at a pace that makes sense for you. You know your body and your mind, so trust your instincts when they tell you to ease up or to push harder. The key is stability — gain stability and control in your movements and the rest will follow. Have patience with yourself and enjoy the *URBAN REBOUNDING* workout.

Conclusion

Reading a book is like taking an imaginary journey. In a work of fiction, the journey is explicitly imaginary, because a world is created which is meant to fully absorb the mind of the reader. A non-fiction work is like a journey too, because an author implicitly asks the reader to follow the contours of an argument with their mind. A conclusion in a work of non-fiction is traditionally a time for the author and the reader to part company. A time to allow the reader to go back to their world and to close up the world of the book. If the book is any good and lasting, a bit of it stays with the reader even after the book is long closed.

This book is a bit different that way. The words on the page can only do so much for the cause. Words on the page are a small part of the journey that needs to be made. The book, I hope, is just a beginning, not really a conclusion at all. The mind could benefit from words only if it translates those words into some kind of action. In the case of *URBAN REBOUNDING*, the body and the mind must be fully engaged with the process at hand.

This book is a means, not an end. I hope the book serves as "skillful means" for you as you embark, or continue with renewed vigor, on your *URBAN REBOUNDING* journey. In great literature there is a certain truth in words—Tolstoy writes and it has a certain resonance with the reader. The mind reverberates by such truth and is drawn to it like a butterfly to a flower.

This book cannot do such a thing because within it is described an activity that must be engaged in with the full body. What I offer is not a lasting literary truth as you conclude this book, but instead, a bodily truth that will resonate within you as you experience the wonder of *URBAN REBOUNDING*. As you close the book, open your mind and open your body, better yet, open up the connection between your mind and your body.

The journey is only a beginning, and the truths are for you to learn as you go on the process of living a full, integrated, healthy life. Allow *URBAN REBOUNDING* to be a part of that full life. The tools are before you, the beginning of a journey awaits you, close this book, and open your life.

APPENDIX A

URBAN REBOUNDING in the Home

Now that you have read the book and are ready to begin *URBAN REBOUNDING* for yourself, there are two items you will need. You will need a well-built rebounder and you will need the *URBAN REBOUNDING* home video. See pages 171-174 to order the *URBAN REBOUNDING* video or additional copies of the *URBAN REBOUNDING* book or the NEEDAK® SOFT-BOUNCE™ rebounder. This is the same high quality NEEDAK® rebounder that J. B. Berns recommends for gym use.

We suggest the video for the reason of the simple maxim, "a picture is worth a thousand words." When it comes to the *URBAN REBOUNDING* workout, moving pictures tell infinitely more! The video will provide you with personal instruction from JB Berns. It will go over technique and each movement in detail. The video also provides the music to the workout so that your rhythm is helped along as you progress on your journey. In *URBAN REBOUNDING*, you are not alone, though your discoveries and triumphs will be intimately your own. I am with you every step of the way, and the video is but one part of this connection. Allow the video and book together to be a guide for you—a beginning.

In time, your own natural rhythmic routines will take over as your body becomes more and more comfortable with itself. You will fold your rebounder up with you and take it to the beach or on vacation, places where a television and VCR are the last thing you want to be around. Relish that time when it comes! But in this beginning time, utilize the *URBAN REBOUNDING* video and let it be a tool of freedom and joy!

APPENDIX B

B

Beyond the Urban Rebounding Workout

In the fitness world today, each dollar spent on equipment, continuing education, or certifications must provide a tremendous return on investment. For Group Fitness, this statement couldn't be truer. No General Manager or Group Fitness Director wants to put forth any amount of money on a new Group Fitness concept that can be out the door as quick as most exercise fads. if all Urban Rebounding had to offer was he 55-minute class described in the previous chapter, we could understand the tentativeness with which you may approach investing in such a program or piece of equipment. This chapter will outline several ways the rebounders can be utilized and the Urban Rebounding concept expanded.

Rebounder as a Personal Training Tool

A piece of equipment that can be transformed from a Group Fitness setting to a one on one situation with ease is a premium in gyms today. Whether your client is in peak physical shape, recovering from minor or major surgery, or you are just searching for a different way to challenge our client cardiovascularly in between strength sets, the rebounder could be just the tool you are looking for.

Sports Specific Training

Ask any athlete what one of the staples of their in-season and off-season training regimen includes and they are sure to answer - plyometrics. Plyometric Training improves an athlete's strength, flexibility, agility and quickness to name a few. If the benefits of plyometric training are so great, why don't we all include it in our workouts? The answer is simple, whether you exercise consistently or not, plyometric training can wreak havoc on joints if not performed on a good surface and with superior form. transforming such plyometric exercises onto the soft surface of the rebounder is a great solution. Quite simply, trainers that have access to a rebounder on the exercise floor can use them for different plyometric drills such as strength moves and sports mimicking exercises rather than having clients perform them on the hard floor.

STRENGTH MOVES
(1) *Squat Jumps* - feet shoulder width apart, hands out in front, bend down into a squat position and explode with straight legs, landing in a squat to complete one repititon
(2) *Squat Jump Variation* - same as above, exploding instead with knees bent into chest
(3) *One Legged Squat Jumps* - same as traditional squat jump, performed with one leg
(4) *One Legged Squat Jump Variation* - same as traditional squat jump, performed with one leg, bringing knees into the chest on jump
(5) *Twisting* - feet shoulder width apart, quick feet action turning body 1/4 turn to either direction and quickly back to starting position; feet stay close to the floor, aim is speed; variations include changing directions, doing 1/2 twists and full turns
(6) *Lateral Hops* - from one side of the Rebounder to the other with feet close together, imagining jumping over a high hurdle; variations include speed and one-foot option
(7) *Forward/Reverse Hops* - from front of the Rebounder to the rear with feet close together, imagining jumping over a high hurdle; variations include speed and one-foot option

SPORTS MIMICKING

(1) *Jump Rope* - feet together in the center, barely leaving the mat to skip the imaginary rope; several variations for jump rope - side to side, forward and back, feet out and in, criss crossing the feet, high knees, butt kicks, heel digs to the front, twisting hips, etc

(2) *Down Hill Skiing* - feet together, arms out to the front to simulate holding poles, jump side to side, feet stay close to mat surface

(3) *Cross Country Skiing* - much like the action on a Nordic Trac, one foot forward and one foot back, opposite arms as legs, alternating legs

(4) *Jogging* - much like jogging in place, the higher the knees come the more intense the drill; variations include delaying (staying on one foot for more than one hop) and sprinting

Circuit Training

As mentioned in Chapter 3, Dr. Kenneth Cooper's Institute of Aerobic Research conducted a study in 1981 heralding the increased strength gains from rebounding in between sets of a weight training circuit. The research states that "strength gains [when rebounding in between circuit weight training] showed a 25% improvement over standard circuit weight training." Whether a personal trainer's goal for their client is increased strength gains, "sneaking" extra cardio into a session, or elevating and sustaining the heart rate throughout a workout, utilizing a rebounder in between sets is the easiest way to get use out of the piece of equipment. Much like a step is used during the Spring Circuit, position a rebounder near machines or equipment you will be using during a training session and have the client perform a basic bounce, jog in place, or another base move in between sets for a specific amount of time. Not only will the activity increase the heart rate and provide cardiovascular training, lactic acid will dissipate enabling the client to train longer and more efficiently (see Chapter 4)

Rehabilitative Clients

Training a client that is returning from injury or illness is always a challenge. What exercises can be performed and at what intensity while keeping the session innovative and interesting? Besides drastically cutting back on intensity and duration during post injury workout, water has always been a standard protocol. However, water is not always a viable option. Rebounding becomes a great tool to use for such clients because of the non-jarring surface of the rebounder, its accessibility and mobility. Any moves that the client performed prior to surgery on the floor, in aerobics class or in training, can be transformed into a workout on the rebounder with 87% less shock to their system. The Needak rebounder utilizes special springs that bow in the middle to further enhance the absorbing properties of the rebounder and lessen the impact on the lower back.

Chapter 5, Therapeutic Rebounding, goes into greater depth regarding training special populations. Elderly exercisers, those that are infirm or wheel chair bound, children, the learning disabled child, people with vision problems, bladder problems, and even those with osteoporosis can benefit from your training on the rebounder. Imagine how your book of business can expand with the knowledge of rebound exercise under your belt.

Resistance Training and the Rebounder

Sand weights are available to be used in conjunction with the Urban Rebounding workout. The sand weights resemble bean-bags, soft and easily held in the hands with a loose grip alleviating any concern of joint problems during exercise. Although the sand weights only weigh either one, two or three pounds a piece, because of the G-force created by jumping on the rebounder, that one pound weight could become considerably heavier depending on the amount of effort put forth by the exerciser [explained further in Chapter 3, page 39].   Standard free weight exercises can be incorporated with the basic bounce if strength gains or upper body sculpting is the focus, or for a total body conditioning workout arm movements simulating free weight exercises may be added to the aerobic moves performed during the Urban Rebounding workout.   The sand weights are not as cumbersome as hand held weights and can be thrown to the ground the moment the participant fatigues.

Speciality Classes Utilizing the Rebounder

The Group Fitness participant of today is much more demanding than a decade ago.   Most participants insist their programs challenge them with innovative classes that can keep their attention for a full hour.   In many cases, that leaves Group Fitness Directors scurrying for the latest fitness craze and trying to implement it all over the schedule.   Then, the participants just grow tired of that and are searching for something new again.   We sometimes overlook the obvious–just mix it up a bit.   Take a new idea and add it in with a tried and true routine such as step or high/low and see how it takes off.   Listed below are some classes based on this idea, taking Urban Rebounding and putting it in other classes to peak their interest but alleviate burn out.

Circuit/Interval Classes

Before Urban Rebounding came along, a favorite at my club was the basic circuit/interval class.   Participants enjoyed doing a standard warm-up followed by alternating segments of step and high/low for an entire hour.   Another spin on the class was adding resistance work in the mix from time to time.   When Urban Rebounding came along we decided to give participants a taste of rebound exercise in these classes.   Instructors would replace one

155

or two segments of high/low with the aerobic portion of the Urban Rebounding class format. The benefits to the trial were endless. First, participants who were comfortable with the circuit/interval format and not very likely to venture out to new classes got a taste of Urban Rebounding. The tease peaked their interest and filled up the standard Urban Rebounding classes. It also gave participants a chance to get used to used to rebounding. As you will find, a 45-minute stint on a rebounder, no matter how basic, is extremely difficult even for your most conditioned person. Also, it takes time for participants to feel comfortable on the rebounder and to master the technique in order to get a superb workout. It also gave instructors that weren't quite ready to go full speed ahead with a 45-55 minute class a chance to hone their skills. Circuit/Interval classes utilizing the rebounders remain on our schedule in addition to the typical Urban Rebounding class format. It's a wonderful introduction to rebound exercise, plus it adds life to your familiar aerobic class.

Recess

Recess is a class that was developed at Crunch Fitness International and serves as a great example of a way the rebounders can be used in different fashion to add a bit of fun to any class. Recess is jus what the name implies, training like you're a kid again. Participants jump rope, run relay races, hula-hoop and hop-scotch, and they might even karate chop a Boppy the Clown or two. The rebounders are used in many ways during this class such as playing hot potato in a circle with playground balls or as part of a circuit.

Box n Bounce

Box n Bounce is another class that was started and Crunch in Atlanta. Kickboxing is the craze at gyms all over the country. However, for the average participant all the kicking , punching and pounding is a bit much on the joints. What better way to make it accessible? Do half of the class on the floor and half on the rebounder. The floor portion of the class is taught, as a traditional Kickboxing class would be. Then, the class transitions to the rebounder and practices the punches while basic bouncing and performing other foot patterns. As participants become comfortable on the rebounder, various kicks are introduced. Sports specific training including plyometrics, strength bounces, and sprinting are mixed in to spice up the workout.

Sculpting

Lower body Sculpting gets a new twist when you put your students on a rebounder to do standard squats, lunges an calf raises. Much like the difference that the Resista Ball makes in exercises. When doing squats on the rebounder, for example, the balance and coordination you must call upon and the different muscles that are utilized to perform stabilization work to complete a simple squat increases the difficulty of the exercise. The same is true for calf raises and lunges (placing either lead leg or trail leg on top of the surface and the other leg on the floor).

Let's not forget the rest of the body and the rebounder. Pushups can be performed with hands firmly on the Permatron® surface. Again, the hands sink into the mat and different muscles are asked to assist in the execution of the move. Triceps dips can be performed using the side of the rebounder as your surface. Abdominal training, as mentioned in the previous chapter regarding the Urban Rebounding workout, can be performed as well.

The greatest benefit to using the rebounder during a sculpting class is that it's there to aid in recovery between sets or when switching from body part to body part. Utilizing the basic bounce at various times during the workout will allow the participant to begin releasing lactic acid and allow him/her to exercise longer and harder, thus experiencing greater benefits over a standard sculpting class.

157

As you can imagine, possibilities are endless on how to use the rebounder for Group Fitness and Personal Training Sessions. I am sure the list will continue to grow exponentially as the use of the Urban Rebounding system continues to expand. Think back to the beginnings of Step, I doubt you or I could have ever imagined all the ways in which that little stepping box would be used to fast forward Group Fitness to where it is today. With creative minds and a diligent pursuit of novel programming, the future seems endless. We at Urban Rebounding will strive to develop and keep you up to date with the newest ideas to keep this piece of equipment you have invested in out of the storage closets and continue there use in Group Fitness rooms across the country.

What are people saying about Urban Rebounding?

"I can find no better aerobic exercise for the physical structure of the human body. Rebounding takes the bone jarring shock out of jogging." - Dr. Gildion Arial, Bio-Mechanical Scientist of the United States Olympic Committee

"Never in my 35 years as a practicing physician have I found an exercise method, for any price, that will do more for the physical body than rebound exercise." - Henry Savage, MD

"This is a workout like no other! I have been a fitness professional for over fifteen years, and JB Berns' Urban Rebounding is the best non-impact cardiovascular workout that I have ever experienced. It's safe, effective and most importantly fun! We have had the program at CRUNCH since September 1998, and all classes are packed nationally." - Donna Cyrus, National Group Fitness Director for CRUNCH Fitness International

"Urban Rebounding is the ultimate aerobic workout; full of energy and excitement and free of shock." - Dr. Art Ulene, Televison's Medical Expert

"Urban Rebounding was the most fun I've had working out in a long time. It's a great anti-stress workout; it doesn't stress your joints and it does de-stress your mind. Best of all it's just pure fun, which is what you need in a workout, so you keep coming back for more." - Tish Hamilton, Managng Editor, Fitness Magazine

"Urban Rebounding is an exciting way to add fun and intensity to my training schedule. Just ask our clients at Revolution Studios in New York." - Terri Walsh, CEO Revolution Studios, NYC

Megan McMorris, writer for Fit Magazine, did a feature on Urban Rebounding in April of 1999: "As we begin jumping, it becomes clear what the class is about. We jog, turn, twist, sprint, kick and box...Although I catch on quickly, the great thing about trampolining [rebouning] is there's always room for improvement. And the class provides that elusive tough-yet-low impact quality...the class's popularity does qualify it as the next Spinning, with one exception: It's fun!"

"I love Urban Rebounding because it's something new! After you've done a really hard workout, you walk away feeling GREAT! And the best part is you know it's easy on your joints." - John Garey, Group Exercise & Pilates Director, Sporting Club at Aventine

"Urban Rebounding is the hottest class around! It's better than Tae Bo... It's like Tae Bo with a bounce." Lisa Druxman, Fitness Director, Sporting Club at Aventine

"Urban Rebounding is the best cardio class! My heart rate peaks and maintains a steady pace and the 'bounce' feels good as well as being safe on my knees and joints. It's a great way to bring fun back into exercise and what a great total body work-out! Basic, fun and challenging; Urban Rebounding is all three!" - Shaon Korte, Group Exercise & Programming Director, Pelican Athletic Club

"Urban Rebounding has added a whole new meaning to our Group Exercise program. Members who have never entered our studios are now doing so to try out this new and exciting pro-gram. Our reqular participants love the added variety Urban Rebounding has contributed to our class schedule. Urban Rebounding is an incredible workout and above all - It is too much fun!" - Doreen Weiserk, Group Exercise Manager, The

Executive Health & Sports Center

"I started Urban Rebounding classes about six weeks ago. The class is almost always full. They love the class. It's fun and they get a grey workout. The word is spreading fast, soon I will be ordering more rebounders. Urban Rebounding has brought people to my facility that would not have come otherwise. It is an asset to my business. Thank you!" - Sherry Macdonald, Owner of Elite Physiques, Inc.

"JB Berns' Urban Rebounding program is straight forward, easy to follow, has no complicated movements, is a fantastic workout and most of all it's safe and it's fun! Our members love it!" - Wendy Zimmerman, Director, Clubs at Woodbridge

"The unique benefits of Urban Rebounding are very simple. It combines an aerobic type workout with an emphasis on balance and coordination. These are the necessary ingredients for teh modern day athlete!" - Diane Lesrah, The Riverview Fitness Center & Racquet Club

Television appearances include Barbara Walter's "The View", Fox Network's news segment "Fox on Health", "The Donnie & Marie Show", "Good Day New York", "Lifetime Network's - Livetime Original", and "Sally Jessy Raphael".

BIBLIOGRAPHY

Bresnick, Edward and Schwartz, Arnold. *Functional Dynamics of the Cell.* New York and London: Academic Press, 1968.

Brooks, Linda. *Rebounding to Better Health.* O'Neill, NE: KE Publishing, 1995.

Carter, Albert E. *The New Miracles of Rebound Exercise.* Fountain Hills, AZ: A.L.M. Publishers, 1988.

The Healthy Cell Seminar. Provo: The American Institute of Reboundology, n.d.

Cooper, Kenneth, H. *Aerobics.* New York: Bantam Books, 1968.

The New Aerobics. New York: Bantam Books, 1970.

Diamond, Harvey and Marilyn. *Fit For Life II: A Complete Health Program.* New York: Warner Books, 1987.

Drinker, Cecil Kent and Yoffey, Joseph Mendel. *Lymphatics, Lymph, and Lymphoid Tissue.* Cambridge, Mass.: Harvard University Press, 1941.

Fife, Bruce. *The Detox Book.* Colorado Springs: HealthWise Publishing and Peccadilly Books, 1997.

Gunthe, Karl, F. *The Physiology of the Cells.* London: The Macmillan Company, 1968.

Guyton, Arthur C. *Textbook of Medical Physiology.* Philadelphia: W.B. Saunders Co., 1976.

Hyams, Joe. *Zen in the Martial Arts.* New York: Bantam Books, 1979.

Lao-Tzu. *The Way of Life.* trans. Witter Bynner. New York: Putnam Publishing Group, 1944.

Martin, Robert. *The Gravity Guiding System*. San Marino, CA: Essential Publishing Co., 1975.

Paul, John. *Cell Biology*. Stanford: Stanford University Press, 1964.

Robbins, Anthony. *Unlimited Power*. New York: Ballantine Books, 1986.

Snieder, Harry and Sarah. *Harry and Sarah Sneider's Olympic Trainer*. Pasadena, CA: Snohomish Publishing Co., 1981.

Solomon, Henry, A. *The Exercise Myth*. New York: Harcourt Brace Javonovich, Publishers, 1984.

Walker, Morton. *Jumping for Health: A Guide to Rebounding Aerobics*. Garden City Park, NY: Avery Publishing Group Inc., 1989

NOTES

Chapter 1

1. Kenneth H. Cooper, M.D., M.P.H., *Aerobics* (New York: Bantam Books, 1968), 1-7. See also Kenneth H. Cooper, *The New Aerobics* (New York: Bantam Books, 1970), 5-15.

2. For a more thorough discussion on notions of disillusionment and unrealistic expectations for exercise programs as they are currently structured please see: Henry A. Solomon, M.D., *The Exercise Myth* (New York: Harcourt Brace Jovanovich, Publishers, 1984), 1-13.

Chapter 2

1. Robert M. Martin, M.D., *The Gravity Guiding System* (San Marino, CA: Essential Publishing Co., 1975), 1-14.

2. Albert E. Carter, *The New Miracles of Rebound Exercise: A Revolutionary* Way to Better Health and Fitness (Fountain Hills, Arizona: A.L.M. Publishers, 1988), 38.

3. Linda Brooks, *Rebounding to Better Health: A Practical Guide to the Ultimate Exercise* (O'Neill, NE: KE Publishing, 1995), 15.

Chapter 3

1. Dr. Morton Walker, *Jumping for Health: A Guide to Rebounding Aerobics* (Garden City Park, NY: Avery Publishing Group, Inc., 1989), 11.

2. *Ibid.*, 13

3. *Ibid.*, 14.

4. *Ibid.*, 14.

5. Carter, *New Miracles of Rebound Exercise*, 25.

6. *Ibid.*, 27, 53.

7. I am drawing exclusively from the 1988 text here because it includes all the information from the 1977 book plus a good deal more detailed research. If anyone is interested in the 1977 book however, it is published by the Reboundology Institute.

8. Carter, *New Miracles of Rebound Exercise*, 124-128.

9. *Ibid.*, 38.

10. *Ibid.*

11. *Ibid.*, 39.

12. *Ibid.*, 39.

13. *Ibid.*, 41.

14. *Ibid.*, 40.

15. *Ibid.*, 41.

16. For an extensive and practical study of this system for athletic and strength training please see *Harry and Sarah Sneider's Olympic Trainer* (Arcadia, CA: Sneider's Family fitness Inc., 1981)

17. Carter, *New Miracles of Rebound Exercise*, 42-44.

18. *Ibid.*, 44.

19. *Ibid.*

20. *Ibid.*, 44-45.

21. *Ibid.*

22. *Ibid.*

23. *Ibid.*, 46.

24. *Ibid.*

25. *Ibid.*, 48.

26. *Ibid.*, 68.

27. *Ibid.*, 68-69.

28. *Ibid.*

29. *Ibid.*, 69-70.

30. *Ibid.*, 71.

31. *Ibid.*, 72.

32. *Ibid.*, 75-76.

33. *Ibid.*, 77.

34. *Ibid.*

35. *Ibid.*, 79-81.

36. *Ibid.* 82.

37. *Ibid.*, 83-84.

38. *Ibid.*, 85-87.

39. *Ibid.*, 108-123.

40. Anthony Robbins, *Unlimited Power* (New York: Ballantine Books, 1986), 172.

41. Marilyn and Harvey Diamond, *Fit For Life II: A Complete Health Program* (New York: Warner Books, 1987), 145-146.

42. Bruce Fife, N.D., *The Detox Book: How to Detoxify Your Body to Improve Your Health, Stop Disease and Reverse Aging* (Colorado Springs: Healthwise Publishing and Peccadilly Books, 1997), 130-131.

43. We will hear directly from *URBAN REBOUNDING* participants in their own words in chapter six of this book

Chapter 4

1. Morton Walker, *Jumping for Health*, 42-45.

2. Linda Brooks, *Rebounding to Better Health*, 15.

3. *Ibid.*, 14.

4. Robert M. Martin, M.D., *The Gravity Guiding System*, 6-7.

5. Albert E. Carter, *The Healthy Cell Seminar* (Provo, Utah: The American Institute of Reboundology, n.d.), 6. and Karl F. Gunthe, *The Physiology of the Cells* (London: The Macmillan Company, 1968), 25-28.

6. Morton Walker, *Jumping for Health*, 62.

7. Albert E. Carter, *Healthy Cell*, 21.

8. *Ibid.*

9. *Ibid.*, 22.

10. Arthur C. Guyton, M.D., *Textbook of Medical Physiology* (Philadelphia: W.B. Saunders Co., 1976), 361.

11. Dr. Morton Walker, *Jumping for Health*, 60.

12. *Ibid.*, 61.

13. *Ibid.*

14. Cecil Kent Drinker and Joseph Mendel Yoffey, *Lymphatics, Lymph, and Lymphoid Tissue* (Cambridge, Mass.: Harvard University Press, 1941), 17-19

15. *Ibid.*, 117.

16. *Ibid.*, 310.

17. Dr. Morton Walker, *Jumping for Health*, 62.

Chapter 5

1. Linda Brooks, *Rebounding to Better Health*, 69.

2. Dr. Robert M. Martin, *The Gravity Guiding System*, 11.

3. Dr. Morton Walker, *Jumping for Health*, 111-112.

4. *Ibid.*, 112.

5. *Ibid.*, 113.

6. Linda Brooks, *Rebounding to Better Health*, 71.

7. *Ibid.*, 72

8. *Ibid.*, 73.

9. Harry and Sarah Sneider, *Harry and Sarah Sneider's Olympic trainer*, 23-29.

10. Dr. Morton Walker, *Jumping For Health*, 130.

11. *Ibid.*, 139.

12. *Ibid.*

13. *Ibid.*, 138.

14. *Ibid.*, 139-140.

15. *Ibid.*, 143.

16. *Ibid.*, 143-144.

17. *Ibid.*, 144.

18. *Ibid.*, 155.

19. *Ibid.*, 160.

20. *Ibid.*

21. *Ibid.*, 161-162.

22. *Ibid.*, 162.

23. *Ibid.*

24. Albert E. Carter, *Healthy Cell*, 82.

25. *Ibid.*, 71.

26. Certain studies have shown that arthritis sufferers may benefit from rebound exercise. I chose not to include a section on the therapeutic benefits of rebounding to heal the pain caused by arthritis and rheumatoid arthritis in the main body of the text due to the complexity of the problem. Nevertheless, rebounding has been shown through personal testimonies to aid in relieving these conditions.

Chapter 6

1. Lao-Tzu, *Tao Te Ching* trans. Witter Bynner (New York: Perigee Books, 1944), 56.

2. *Ibid.*, 47

3. *Ibid.*, 104.

Chapter 7

1. The source of all of these bounces come from Albert E. Carter's pioneering work regarding the most efficient way to move on the rebound unit. I use the bounces differently with regard to the specifics of the *URBAN REBOUNDING* technique and its relationship to the martial arts, but nevertheless, Carter's work stands as my ultimate source material. The original source can be found in: Albert E. Carter, New Miracles, 95-107.